COOKBOOK FOR BEGINNERS

VEGAN DIET ESSENTIALS WITH OVER 100 PLANT-POWERED SATISFYING VEGAN RECIPES FOR WEIGHT LOSS, ENERGY AND VIBRANT HEALTH

Disclaimer

The information in this book is not to be used as medical advice. The recipes should be used in combination with guidance from your physician. Please consult your physician before beginning any diet. It is especially important for those with diabetes, and those on medications to consult with their physician before making changes to their diet.

Introduction

Every day, we make conscious choices. These everyday choices may seem so minute, so unimportant. However, they're in fact not only affecting the state of our planetary environment; they're affecting our physical health.

As vegans, we do something extraordinary: we choose to live in a caring, more humane world.

We choose to heighten our nutrition with everything that grows from the green earth beneath us, without choosing to damage it in the process. We choose to fill our plates with color, with vibrancy—rather than turning back to the old and burdened way of eating grocer-packaged meat, of eating cows that have been annihilated after their "purpose" on the farm is done or eating animals that have been bred and born only to die and spread out on our tables.

This book centers around the health of the vegan diet because choosing to refute meat, cheese, and other animal-laden products opens your body to the wonderful benefits and the nutrients of the earth. Vegan diets are stripped of cholesterol and are very low in saturated fat. So turning toward this path puts your heart literally at ease and decreases your risk of heart attack and stroke as well as many other diseases.

Many people would love to adopt the vegan way of life however due to the uncertainty of where to start, they're frozen in the grocery store, unsure of what to purchase. After all the history of the vegan diet is not a long one, as I'll demonstrate later. It can be difficult to begin a new diet especially when you have been eating a certain way for years. Do not despair, this book will guide you from where to find the protein sources to making sure you have everything you need on your shopping list.

In addition, this book takes you on a journey: a journey to understand the immense benefits of the vegan diet; a journey to help you make the switch from "going with the flow" to choosing to live well. If you're confused about the "protein situation," we've got you covered here; your muscles and metabolism (and brain) will thank you.

The benefits of the vegan diet are endless. You will increase your nutrient intake. You will decrease your risk of very serious diseases and cancers. You will also increase your energy and slim your waistline. Do all of this while making environmentally-conscious decisions about what you eat. Don't allow yourself to promote the meat industry another day.

Enjoy the following 100 vegan recipes— each packed with nutrition and powerful vegan benefits. Enjoy your new, conscious, and harmonic life!

Table of Contents

 **CHAPTER 1**

A VEGAN DIET
INTRODUCTION

The vegan diet is a powerful one: one that looks at the animal-cruel, and unhealthy meat and dairy industries with an evil eye. Learn more about how you can make the switch today.

History of the Vegan Diet

Despite the fact that "veganism" seems a bit like a fad of the twenty-first century (with vegan food even popping up at pubs and late-night diners), the vegan lifestyle has actually been around for many centuries. People began to refute animal products approximately two thousand years ago. Around 500 B.C.E., Greek philosopher Pythagoras chose vegetarianism and discussed the fact that people should live in greater harmony alongside the creatures of the earth. Furthermore, Buddha turned toward the vegetarian diet, yielding many centuries of Indian vegetarian dieters.

The modern day revolution of the vegan diet came in 1944—a good number of years after Buddha promoted it in the B.C.E. A man named Donald Watson brought together several other vegetarians who also did not eat dairy. They discussed their lifestyle, as well as a new name for themselves. They filtered through benevore, dairyban, and several others before finalizing "vegan." These were the initial Vegan Society folks, and their message has spread wildly over the United States and Canada, with many people refuting dairy and animal products all together.

Benefits of the Vegan Diet

The health benefits of going vegan are staggering. While the rest of the world continues to pummel their veins with saturated fats, their minds with animal product-garbage, the vegan dieters turn toward from-the-earth ingredients and fuel themselves with bountiful nutrition.

1. The Vegan Diet Has Immense Nutritional Benefits

The vegan diet is pulsing with nuts, vegetables, fruits, whole grains, soy products, and legumes such as beans. These ingredients offer good, bountiful carbohydrates, which your body requires for energy. If your body doesn't get enough carbohydrates, it turns toward your muscle to gain energy. This, in turn, makes you feel weak.

Furthermore, the vegan diet provides miniscule amounts of saturated fats. The incredible amount of saturated fat found in animal products puts people at risk for serious cardiovascular diseases such as heart attack and stroke.

The vegan diet is pulsing with fiber, which fights against colon cancer and further makes you feel fuller for longer. This is another reason the vegan dieter is generally slimmer than the average, animal product consuming person.

The vegan diet contains a good deal of folate, which is a B vitamin that generates cell growth and repair. It works to heal your cells and prevents premature aging; it also protects your body against certain cancers.

Note that the vegan diet is of course, very plant-based and thus it contains many phytochemicals. These phytochemicals fight back against cancer growth, boost enzyme productivity, and promote overall cell growth.

Furthermore, the vegan diet offers protein in the form of beans, lentils, peas, and many soy products. Remember that the regular Western diet contains far too much protein, which is found in highly consumed steaks and hamburgers. However, when you eat these nutrient-rich earth products, your intake of protein is sufficient and you put yourself at decreased risk of many diseases.

2. The Vegan Diet Refutes Many Dangerous Elements of the Typical Western Diet

As already mentioned, the typical Western diet contains far too much protein. In addition, it further turns towards many other dangerous products that put people at risk of obesity and other serious health issues.

For example, eggs, consumed by millions on almost a daily basis, contain far too much cholesterol. This cholesterol can ramp up the cholesterol in people's blood streams, putting them at risk for heart disease, heart attack, and stroke.

Americans also eat far too much sugar, which puts them at risk for diabetes and obesity. However, most vegans understand that processed sugar, found in nearly every packaged item on shelves all over the continent, is made utilizing activated charcoal.

What's activated charcoal? Activated charcoal is made from animal bones.

Furthermore, the sheer fact that most of the world—over seventy-five percent, to be exact—is lactose intolerant makes it very, very unlikely that Americans should be drinking cow's milk at all. Most people have milk sensitivities, but they live their lives undiagnosed.

The typical American diet hones in on meat, as you know. However, did you know that many of the animals you consume from the grocery store were initially given hormones in order to help them grow faster? This means that every time a person eats an animal that was given these terrorizing hormones, he's disrupting the very delicate balance of his bodily hormones. This can lead to unnecessary weight gain and potential cancers.

3. The Vegan Diet is Much Kinder to the Earth.

As I've continually mentioned, the vegan diet is very much a harmonious, humane diet that takes notice and cares for the environment. Simply put, going vegan eases your conscience, as it doesn't alter any animal's life so that you can live more easily. It's a selfless diet.

Growing plants in the earth takes far fewer resources than taming and feeding animals. You're taking soft steps on the planet, rather than pounding your feet into the ground, declaring it your own. We're only here for a little while. Remember that.

Vegan Diet and Protein: Where to Find It?

If you're considering the vegan diet, most likely you've had several people approach you with the classic question: "Where do you think you're going to get your protein?"

In order to create one protein, you require 20 amino acids. Nine of these amino acids must be found in the external environment—meaning your body can't produce them on its own. When people talk about the term "complete protein," they're talking about a food that contains all nine of these amino acids. Generally, meat and eggs are complete proteins, while many vegan diet mainstays are not.

However, vegan diets contain such a wide array of amino acids that we don't need to seek "complete" proteins. Rather, we can chip away at the amino acid profile throughout the many hours of our day in order to stock up on proteins.

Fortunately, you can also find a good deal of complete proteins while on the vegan diet. You just have to know where to look! Check out this vegan complete protein list below:

Buckwheat: 6 grams of complete proteins per 1 cup serving.

Quinoa: 8 grams of complete proteins per 1 cup serving.

Chia Seeds: 4 grams of complete proteins per 2 tbsp. serving.

Rice PLUS Beans: 7 grams of complete proteins per 1 cup serving.

Seitan: 21 grams of complete protein per 1/3 cup serving.

*Note: Gluten-haters state that seitan is the devil. (After all, it is a gluten protein.) However, if you don't have a gluten allergy, you must know that this Chinese Buddhist monk recipe is simply delicious and vital to your health. Just look at all that protein!

Spirulina: 4 grams of complete protein per 1 tbsp. serving.

Hempseed: 10 grams of complete protein per 2 tbsp. serving.

Soy: 10 grams of complete protein per ½ cup serving.

**Note: Soy is what makes tofu the perfect protein substitute!

Tempeh: 31 grams complete protein per 1 cup serving.

Making the Vegan Leap: Tips to Transition Smoothly

Because you've most likely grown up on an animal product-eating American diet, transitioning into the vegan lifestyle might take a bit of time. However, know that this transition is one of the most beneficial things you'll ever do in your life. (So stay strong!)

Follow these tips in order to assimilate into this new lifestyle, live well, and feel confident in your choices.

1. Stock Your Shelves.

This first step asks you to head to the store (on your normal grocery day), and stock up on VEGAN foods. These foods are delicious and vibrant—providing so many colors and so many different textures, you'll be amazed. During your trip, think of all the things you're buying, rather than thinking of all the things you're leaving OUT! (That chicken, beef, etc.)

2. Check Out a Few Pro-Vegan Films.

As you educate yourself on the vegan diet, it's important that you get excited about it as well! Documentaries like Hungry for Change or Food Inc. make you ANGRY about the way the world is and pump you up to make a change. When you switch to the vegan lifestyle, you're making a 'soulful' change, from the comfort of your own home. Just one single person can do so much to help the planet.

3. Start with the Basics and Work Your Way Up!

Don't start with processed vegan foods. Rather, eat wholesome, nutritious, and filling vegan foods—foods from the earth. This way, you'll feel more satisfied. You won't be "cheating" right away (with things like non-dairy coconut ice cream which, to be honest, is delicious and allowed on occasion, of course).

4. Don't Over-Do It At First.

When you're first starting the vegan diet, it can be easy to get carried away with preparing every meal with wonderful ingredients and spices. However, if you do this for every meal—taking two hours every afternoon and evening to prepare something really special—you'll get burned out. You can instead focus on simple things, like rice or pasta, occasionally. Just make sure to always toss vegetables into every meal!

Vegan Diet Shopping List

Heading to the store as a novice Vegan dieter can be a bit overwhelming. Check out the following shopping list—which includes the ingredients necessary for most of the 100 vegan recipes in this book!

Vegetables:
Onions
Spinach
Kale
Broccoli
Green peppers
Red peppers
Zucchini
Sweet potatoes
Yukon potatoes
Red potatoes
Butternut squash
Carrots
Etc.

Fruits:
Apples
Pineapples

Cherries
Strawberries
Mangoes
Avocadoes
Bananas
Blueberries
Etc.

Grains:
Rice
Quinoa
Barley
Buckwheat
Lentils
Pastas

Cupboard Snacks:
Cashews
Almonds
Peanut Butter
Pistachios
Dried Fruit

Vegan essentials:
Olive oil
Coconut oil
Nutritional Yeast

Almond milk
Maple syrup
Honey
Chickpeas
Kidney beans

Vegan Diet Substitutions for Easy Swapping

Sometimes, you might need to swap out the "old" to initiate with the new vegan diet. Here are a few of my favorite swaps.

Butter Substitutes:

Check out Earth Balance, the vegan butter. They have incredible vegan butters, with many different options.

Milk Substitutes:

Soymilk, Almond milk, Rice milk or Coconut milk are all good options.

"Meat" Substitutes:

If you aren't into seitan, tempeh, or tofu, you might try the Gardein products, Amy's Frozen grocery products, Field Roast products, or Tofurkey.

Cream Cheese Substitute:

Try Tofutti Cream Cheese!

Cheese Substitutes:

I recommend Diaya's Mozzarella, Cheddar, and Parmesan.

Vegan Ricotta from Nutty Cow is delectable.

Furthermore, turn toward nutritional yeast (found in many of the following recipes!) for a nutty, near-cheese flavor. It's delicious!

Now, get ready for the following 100 VEGAN RECIPES!

CHAPTER 2

VEGAN BREAKFAST RECIPES

Fiber-Rich Oatmeal and Blueberry Waffles

Recipe Makes 6 Servings.

Prep Time: 12 minutes.
Cook Time: 4 minutes.

Nutritional Information Per Serving: 460 calories, 55 grams carbohydrates, 25 grams fat, 7 grams protein.

Ingredients:
1 ¼ cup flour
½ tsp. sea salt
1 tsp. baking powder
1 ¼ cup oats
½ cup applesauce, unsweetened
½ tsp. cinnamon
2 cups almond milk
2 tbsp. olive oil
4 tbsp. maple syrup
2 cups blueberries, frozen
1 tsp. vanilla

Directions:

Add the dry ingredients into a medium-sized mixing bowl. Stir well.

Create a hole in the center of the dry ingredients, and add all the wet ingredients. Stir the mixture until it's just combined, making sure not to over stir.

Allow the mixture to thicken, without touching it, for a full ten minutes.

Add the blueberries at this time.

Pour about a half cup of the batter into the waffle iron at a time. Cook the waffles according to the waffle iron instructions, and enjoy with a bit more maple syrup and fresh fruit!

Tofu-Based Omelet

Recipe Makes 2 Servings.

Prep Time: 8 minutes.
Cook Time: 30 minutes.

Nutritional Information Per Serving: 258 calories, 16 grams carbohydrates, 20 grams protein, 15 grams fat.

Ingredients:
9 ounces tofu, firm, patted dry
4 minced garlic cloves
3 tbsp. hummus
½ tsp. salt
½ tsp. pepper
3 tbsp. nutritional yeast
½ tsp. paprika
1 tbsp. arrowroot powder
¼ cup diced onion
¼ cup diced mushrooms
½ cup spinach
1 tbsp. olive oil

Directions:

Begin by preheating the oven to 375 degrees Fahrenheit.

Prepare the vegetables and drain and dry out the tofu. Set these ingredients to the side.

Heat a skillet over medium-high heat. Add the olive oil to the mixture, and sauté the garlic for three minutes.

Add garlic to the food processor. Add the tofu and the arrowroot to the food processor, and process the ingredients well. In order to thin the ingredients, add approximately 2 tbsp. of water. Set this mixture to the side.

Next, heat the skillet over medium heat. Add the remaining vegetables, and sauté for approximately four minutes. Set the mixture to the side.

Remove the vegetables from the skillet. Smear the tofu mixture over the bottom of the skillet, making sure to spread it evenly and gently. It should be thin, without any holes.

Next, cook the mixture over medium for six minutes. Place the skillet in the preheated oven and allow the omelet to bake for approximately thirteen minutes.

With three minutes left on the omelet's cook time, add the vegetables back to the top of the omelet. Allow the vegetables to cook with the omelet for the remaining amount of time.

Remove the omelet from the stove, and fold the omelet over carefully. Serve the omelet, and enjoy!

Monkey's Paw Banana Bread

Recipe Makes 6 Servings.

Prep Time: 20 minutes.
Cook Time: 40 minutes.

Nutritional Information Per Serving: 396 calories, 55 grams carbohydrates, 18 grams fat, 5 grams protein.

Ingredients:
3 small and mashed bananas
½ cup black coffee, the liquid brewed
6 tbsp. water
3 tbsp. flax seed (allowed to sit with the water for ten minutes)
½ cup olive oil
½ cup brown sugar
1 cup flour
¾ cup whole-wheat flour
½ tsp. sea salt
2 tsp. baking powder
1 tsp. nutmeg
½ tsp. allspice

Directions:

Begin by preheating the oven to 350 degrees Fahrenheit.

Stir together the olive oil and the sugar. To the side, place the flax seed and the water together in a small bowl and allow it to sit for ten minutes. Add this mixture to the olive oil and the sugar, and stir well.

Add the coffee and the bananas. Next, add the salt, flours, and the remaining spices and baking powders.

Make sure to fold in the dry ingredients, rather than stirring them with vigor.

Pour the mixture into a bread pan, and allow the bread to bake for forty minutes. The bread should be browned on its top.

Tuscan Vegan Quiche

Recipe Makes 6 Servings.

Prep Time: 30 minutes.
Cook Time: 50 minutes.

Nutritional Information Per Serving: 304 calories, 21 grams carbohydrates, 19 grams fat, 11 grams protein.

Ingredients:
Crust Ingredients:
3 tbsp. water
1 tbsp. chia seeds, allowed to sit with the water for ten minutes
1 cup oats, ground into flour
1 cup almond flour
1 tsp. oregano
1 tsp. parsley
½ tsp. thyme
1 tbsp. olive oil
½ tsp. salt
3 tbsp. water

Quiche Ingredients:

14 ounces tofu, firm

1 diced onion

1 tbsp. olive oil

1 cup spinach

4 minced garlic cloves

2 ½ cups sliced mushrooms

½ cup diced sun-dried tomatoes

1 cup diced chives

1 tsp. sea salt

3 tbsp. nutritional yeast

Directions:

Begin by preheating the oven to 350 degrees Fahrenheit.

Next, press the tofu to remove the water.

To make the crust, stir together the water and the chia seeds and allow them to sit together for ten minutes.

Next, stir together the spices, almond flour, and the oat flour—made in the food processor.

Next, add the oil and the chia seed mixture. Stir well, making sure to add 1 tbsp. of water at a time in order to create the texture of "cookie dough."

Place the dough onto the bottom of a pie pan. Press at the dough in order to make it thin.

Bake the quiche crust for a full fifteen minutes. The quiche crust should be golden. At this time, boost the temperature up twenty-five degrees, to 375 degrees Fahrenheit.

Now, create your quiche filling. Place the tofu in the food processor, and process the tofu until it's creamy. In order to help it become appropriately creamy, you can add a bit of almond milk.

Place the onion and the olive oil in a skillet. Add the garlic, and cook the ingredients over medium-high heat for three minutes. Add the mushrooms, and cook the mixture for twelve minutes. Add the herbs, spinach, tomatoes, spices, and the nutritional yeast. Cook for three minutes more.

At this time, remove the skillet from the heat. Add the tofu to the mixture, and stir well. Pour this mixture over the quiche crust, and smooth the mixture until it's completely even.

Next, bake the quiche for thirty-five minutes at 375 degrees Fahrenheit. The quiche should be incredibly firm.

After you remove the quiche from the oven, you should allow it to cool for twenty minutes.

Andes Mountain Cinnamon Quinoa Oatmeal

Recipe Makes 4 Servings.

Prep Time: 10 minutes.
Cook Time: 25 minutes.

Nutritional Information Per Serving: 390 calories, 57 grams carbohydrates, 16 grams fat, 8 grams protein.

Ingredients:
1 cup water
3/ 4 cup almond milk
1 cup rinsed quinoa
1 tsp. cinnamon
2 ½ cups blackberries
½ cup pecans, diced
5 tsp. agave

Directions:
Bring the quinoa, water, and the almond milk together in a medium-sized saucepan. Boil the ingredients over high heat.

When the mixture begins to boil, cover the mixture and reduce the heat to low.

Allow the mixture to simmer for twenty minutes. The liquid should be absorbed into the quinoa.

Turn off the heat and allow the quinoa to rest for six minutes, still covered.

Add the blackberries and the cinnamon at this time. Portion out the servings, and add the pecans overtop.

Add the agave nectar to the top of each bowl of quinoa, and enjoy!

Warm Soul Breakfast Lentils

Recipe Makes 6 Servings.

Prep Time: 5 minutes.
Cook Time: 65 minutes.

Nutritional Information Per Serving: 158 calories, 17 grams carbohydrates, 7 grams fat, 5 grams protein.

Ingredients:
1 diced onion
3 tbsp. olive oil
2 minced garlic cloves
¾ cup green lentils
2 ½ cups water
1 tbsp. tomato paste
1 ½ tbsp. soy sauce
½ tsp. salt
½ tsp. pepper

Directions:
Pour the olive oil into a medium-sized saucepan and heat it over medium heat.

Add the onion, tomato paste, and garlic.
Stir and cook for about five minutes.

At this time, add the lentils and the water.
Bring the water to a boil.

When the water comes to a boil, reduce
the heat to medium-low, cover the
saucepan, and allow the mixture to
simmer. Stir every few minutes until the
lentils are completely tender. This should
take approximately fifty minutes.

Next, remove the saucepan from the heat
and allow it to sit for ten minutes,
covered.

Add the salt, the pepper, and the soy
sauce at this time. Serve warm, and enjoy!

Vegan French Toast

Recipe Makes 6 Servings.

Prep Time: 12 minutes.
Cook Time: 6 minutes.

Nutritional Information Per Serving: 338 calories, 53 grams carbohydrates, 9 grams fat, 9 grams protein.

Ingredients:
6 slices of vegan bread of your choice, I used ciabatta (each sliced thin, approximately 1/2-inch)
2 tbsp. maple syrup
¾ cup almond milk
1 tbsp. nutritional yeast
3 tbsp. flour
½ tsp. nutmeg
1 tsp. cinnamon
½ tsp. salt
Olive oil for frying

Directions:

Begin by stirring together the maple syrup, almond milk, yeast, nutmeg, cinnamon, and salt.

Next, place the sliced bread in a baking dish in a single layer. Pour the initial mixture overtop the bread, making sure to coat it thoroughly on both sides.

Heat the olive oil in a big skillet over medium-high heat.

When the oil gets hot, cook the bread slices in the oil for about three minutes on each side. The bread should be golden.

Serve with a bit of extra maple syrup, and enjoy!

Walk Like an Egyptian Vegan Breakfast

Recipe Makes 4 Servings.

Prep Time: 12 hours.
Cook Time: 35 minutes.

Nutritional Information Per Serving: 390 calories, 52 grams carbohydrates, 12 grams fat, 22 grams protein.

Ingredients:
5 minced garlic cloves
¾ pound dried fava beans (rounded, rather than flat)
1 tsp. cumin
½ tsp. sea salt
3 tbsp. olive oil
2 lemons
½ cup fresh parsley leaves

Directions:
Rinse the fava beans and cover the beans with water. Soak them overnight.

Next, drain the beans. Add them to a saucepan, and add one inch of water over the top. Bring the beans to a boil and cook until they're completely tender, approximately thirty minutes. Know that you can add more water as needed.

Drain the beans. Keep the liquid from the bean mixture for a later step.

Next, toss the fava beans with the olive oil, garlic, and salt.

Portion out the bean mixture into the various bowls, and then pour a bit of the bean broth over the top of the beans. Add more olive oil, if you like.

Add lemon juice, parsley, and some pepper, if you please. Enjoy!

Vegan Coconut Porridge

Recipe Makes 4 Servings.

Prep Time: 40 minutes.
Cook Time: 25 minutes.

Nutritional Information Per Serving: 215 calories, 25 grams carbohydrates, 13 grams fat, 2 grams protein.

Ingredients:
½ cup white sugar
1/3 cup tapioca, small pearl
2 cups water
13 ounces coconut milk
1/3 cup coconut flakes, unsweetened and toasted

Directions:
Place the water and the tapioca into a medium-sized saucepan. Allow the tapioca to soak for forty minutes.

At this time, add the sugar and the coconut milk. Boil the mixture over medium, making sure to stir all the time.

Place the heat on low. Cook for another twenty minutes. The tapioca should be clear.

Add the coconut flakes, and portion out. Enjoy!

Garbanzo Pancakes

Recipe Makes 2 Servings.

Prep Time: 10 minutes.
Cook Time: 10 minutes.

Nutritional Information Per Serving: 60 calories, 12 grams carbohydrates, 1 gram fat, 3 grams protein.

Ingredients:
½ cup garbanzo bean flour
1 diced onion
1/3 cup diced red pepper
½ tsp. black pepper
½ tsp. salt
½ tsp. garlic powder
½ cup water
½ tsp. baking powder

Directions:
To start, dice up the vegetables and preheat a large skillet over medium.

Next, stir together the spices, the garbanzo flour, and the baking powder in a medium-sized mixing bowl. Add the water, and stir well to remove all clumps.

Add the diced vegetables.

When the skillet is completely heated, coat it with olive oil.

Pour the batter into the skillet, and spread it out well to create a flattened pancake. Cook it for approximately seven minutes on the first side, and then flip it. Cook for an additional four minutes. Both sides should be golden brown. Make sure to watch it!

Serve the garbanzo pancake, and enjoy!

🍴 CHAPTER

3

VEGAN JUICE AND SMOOTHIE RECIPES

Carrot Ginger Juice

Recipe Makes 2 Servings.

Prep Time: 5 minutes.
Cook Time: 0 minutes.

Nutritional Information Per Serving: 57 calories, 12 grams carbohydrates, 1 gram fat, 2 grams protein.

Ingredients:
2 peeled cucumbers
½ cup carrots, baby
1 trimmed beet
1 lime, with skin
2-inch piece of ginger, diced

Directions:
Be sure to prepare the vegetables into small, easily juiced portions. It's best to chop the vegetables right before juicing so as to retain the nutrients and vitamins; chopped vegetables tend to lose their nutrients as the juices leave them from the gaping holes.

Bring the pieces through the juicer. If the pulp that is transmitted into the pulp basket is still wet, run the pulp through an additional time. Your pulp should be completely dry so as not to waste any of the juice.

Mango-Based Grapefruit Smoothie

Recipe Makes 2 Servings.

Prep Time: 5 minutes.
Cook Time: 0 minutes.

Nutritional Information Per Serving: 224 calories, 54 grams carbohydrates, 1 gram fat, 3 grams protein.

Ingredients:
2 peeled and sliced mangoes
2 grapefruits, peeled and segmented
Juice from 1 grapefruit

Directions:
Bring all the ingredients together into a blender. Blend well, and enjoy!

Banana-Based Mango Basil Smoothie

Recipe Makes 4 Servings.

Prep Time: 10 minutes.
Cook Time: 0 minutes.

Nutritional Information Per Serving: 384 calories, 33 grams carbohydrates, 27 grams fat, 4 grams protein.

Ingredients:
2 bananas, frozen
1 ½ peeled and sliced mangoes
3 sliced carrots
2 cups almond milk
5 basil leaves
4 ice cubes

Directions:
Bring all the ingredients in a blender and blend until smooth. Enjoy!

Garlic and Spinach-Based Tomato Juice

Recipe Makes 2 Servings.

Prep Time: 5 minutes.
Cook Time: 0 minutes.

Nutritional Information Per Serving: 102 calories, 24 grams carbohydrates, 1 gram fat, 5 grams protein.

Ingredients:
3 garlic cloves
4 cups tomato juice
3 tsp. cilantro
4 tbsp. onion, diced
½ cup spinach
½ tsp. red pepper flakes
½ tsp. cumin

Directions:
Bring all the above ingredients together in a blender. Blend until completely smooth. Enjoy!

Apple Pie of My Eye Green Smoothie

Recipe Makes 2 Servings.

Prep Time: 5 minutes.
Cook Time: 0 minutes.

Nutritional Information Per Serving: 367 calories, 52 grams carbohydrates, 17 grams fat, 6 grams protein.

Ingredients:
1 cup water
3 tbsp. walnuts
1 cup apple juice, unsweetened and organic
1 tsp. maple syrup
½ tsp. nutmeg
½ tsp. cinnamon
4 cups spinach
1 peeled cucumber
2 diced apples
½ diced avocado, frozen
10 ice cubes

Directions:

Bring the above ingredients into a blender. Blend the ingredients for approximately one minute, until completely smooth. Enjoy!

Gluten-Free Blueberry Vanilla Muffin Smoothie

Recipe Makes 2 Servings.

Prep Time: 5 minutes.
Cook Time: 0 minutes.

Nutritional Information Per Serving: 371 calories, 15 grams carbohydrates, 32 grams fat, 10 grams protein.

Ingredients:
3 cups almond milk, vanilla flavored
4 tbsp. gluten-free oats or quinoa flakes
1 cup blueberries
2 tbsp. chia seeds
2 tsp. vanilla
3 tbsp. vanilla protein powder, soy

Directions:
The evening before you wish to consume this wonderful smoothie, bring all the ingredients together in a large glass or pitcher. Stir the ingredients, and place the mixture in the refrigerator overnight.

When morning comes, pour the ingredients into a blender, and blend the mixture until smooth. Enjoy!

Kale Lemonade

Recipe Makes 2 Servings.

Prep Time: 5 minutes.
Cook Time: 0 minutes.

Nutritional Information Per Serving: 377 calories, 95 grams carbohydrates, 1 gram fat, 5 grams protein.

Ingredients:
2 bushels kale (de-stemmed)
4 celery stalks
2 green apples
2 cucumbers, sliced
4 cups lemonade

Directions:
Bring the above ingredients together into a blender. Blend until smooth, and enjoy!

Spiced Autumn Smoothie

Recipe Makes 2 Servings.

Prep Time: 5 minutes.
Cook Time: 0 minutes.

Nutritional Information Per Serving: 210 calories, 30 grams carbohydrates, 10 grams fat, 3 grams protein.

Ingredients:
2 cups almond milk, vanilla flavored
1 banana, frozen
1 cup pumpkin, canned
½ tsp. ginger
1 tsp. maple syrup
½ tsp. cinnamon
1 tsp. vanilla
½ tsp. nutmeg

Directions:
Bring together all the ingredients in a blender, and blend until smooth. Enjoy!

Chocolate Delight Spirulina Green Smoothie

Recipe Makes 2 Servings.

Prep Time: 5 minutes.
Cook Time: 0 minutes.

Nutritional Information Per Serving: 410 calories, 40 grams carbohydrates, 27 grams fat, 7 grams protein.

Ingredients:

2 cups spinach
2 cups almond milk
3 tbsp. coconut oil
1 tbsp. almond butter
3 tbsp. cocoa powder
2 tsp. spirulina
2 tbsp. agave syrup
2 cups frozen blueberries
10 ice cubes

Directions:

Bring the ingredients into a blender, and blend the ingredients well until completely smooth. Enjoy!

Zesty Lime Smoothie

Recipe Makes 2 Servings.

Prep Time: 5 minutes.
Cook Time: 0 minutes.

Nutritional Information Per Serving: 280 calories, 50 grams carbohydrates, 11 grams fat, 7 grams protein.

Ingredients:
Zest from 3 limes
4 tbsp. lime juice
½ tsp. vanilla
2 bananas, frozen
2 cups almond milk
2 tbsp. almond butter
1 date, pitted
4 cups spinach
8 ice cubes

Directions:
Bring the ingredients into a blender, and blend until smooth. Enjoy!

CHAPTER

VEGAN APPETIZERS, DIPS, AND SNACKS

4

Mid-Day Avocado Quesadillas

Recipe Makes 6 Servings.

Prep Time: 5 minutes.
Cook Time: 10 minutes.

Nutritional Information Per Serving: 247 calories, 26 grams carbohydrates, 14 grams fat, 5 grams protein.

Ingredients:
4 diced onions
6 8-inch flour tortillas
1 ½ diced avocadoes
2 cups grated vegan cheese, I like Daiya or another homemade version

Directions:
Spread the tortillas over the counter, and divide the grated cheese overtop. Add the remaining ingredients, the onions and the avocadoes, as well.

At this time, fold each of the quesadillas in half. Grill the quesadillas on a preheated griddle, making sure to flip them when

their initial side is already golden. This
should be about five minutes on each side.

Serve the quesadillas in wedges, and
enjoy!

Garlic Bean Dip

Recipe Makes 6 Servings.

Prep Time: 2 minutes.
Cook Time: 0 minutes.

Nutritional Information Per Serving: 284 calories, 43 grams carbohydrates, 5 grams fat, 16 grams protein.

Ingredients:
4 minced garlic cloves
15 ounces white beans
3 tbsp. lemon juice
2 tbsp. olive oil
1 tsp. cumin
1 tsp. salt
4 drops hot pepper sauce
1 tsp. chili powder

Directions:
Bring all the above ingredients into a food processor, and process the ingredients until completely smooth. This should take about two minutes.

Know that if your mixture is far too chunky, add water slowly as it processes to reach your desired consistency. Enjoy with veggie sticks or organic tortilla chips!

Tofu and Garbanzo Garlic Hummus

Recipe Makes 6 Servings.

Prep Time: 4 minutes.
Cook Time: 0 minutes.

Nutritional Information Per Serving: 371 calories, 46 grams carbohydrates, 13 grams fat, 19 grams protein.

Ingredients:
1 ½ tbsp. olive oil
1 cup diced tofu, firm
15 ounces garbanzo beans
¼ cup lemon juice
3 tbsp. peanut butter
5 minced garlic cloves

Directions:
Add all above ingredients to a food processor. Process well until smooth.

Chill the hummus, and serve with vegetables. Enjoy!

Vegan Nachos

Recipe Makes 6 Servings.

Prep Time: 5 minutes.

Cook Time: 20 minutes.

Nutritional Information Per Serving: 273 calories, 36 grams carbohydrates, 12 grams fat, 5 grams protein.

Ingredients:
12 corn tortillas
3 diced jalapeno peppers
1 diced onion
3 tsp. olive oil
2 diced garlic cloves
3 diced tomatoes
3 tbsp. rice milk
8 ounces grated vegan cheddar cheese

Directions:
Preheat the oven to 375 degrees Fahrenheit.

At this time, slice up the corn tortillas into small wedges. Place them on a baking sheet, and allow them to bake for twenty minutes.

Next, heat the onion and garlic in a skillet with olive oil. Sauté for approximately five minutes.

Then add the jalapenos and tomatoes, sautéing for another minute. Add the rice milk.

Now, add the vegan cheese to the mixture and stir well. The mixture should be melted. Remove the mixture from the heat.

Spread the oven-cooked tortillas onto a big platter, and pour the cheese sauce over the nachos. Enjoy!

Tofu Chicken Nuggets

Recipe Makes 6 Servings.

Prep Time: 5 minutes.
Cook Time: 30 minutes.

Nutritional Information Per Serving: 177 calories, 21 grams carbohydrates, 6 grams fat, 11 grams protein.

Ingredients:
30 ounces firm tofu
1 ¼ cup barbecue sauce

Directions:
Preheat the oven to 420 degrees Fahrenheit.

Next, slice the tofu into small, chicken nugget-sized pieces. Blot at the tofu with a paper towel to remove the water. Press the tofu well to completely remove the liquid.

Add the tofu to the vegan barbecue sauce, and stir well. Place the tofu on a baking sheet.

Allow the tofu to bake for fifteen minutes. At this time, stir the tofu, and then bake for another twelve minutes. Enjoy!

Indian Samosas

Recipe Makes 6 Servings.

Prep Time: 5 minutes.
Cook Time: 25 minutes.

Nutritional Information Per Serving: 323 calories, 45 grams carbohydrates, 14 grams fat, 5 grams protein.

Ingredients:
3 diced onions
1/3 cup olive oil
4 tsp. curry powder
1 tsp. mustard seeds
3 diced potatoes
2 diced carrots
½ cup diced green beans
8 ounces phyllo pastry
½ cup water
Olive oil for frying

Directions:
Heat the olive oil in a medium-sized skillet. Add the mustard seeds, heating them over medium heat until they pop.

Add the onion and cook for another six minutes.

Add the salt, and the curry powder at this time. Fry these ingredients for two minutes.

Add the potatoes, carrots, beans, and water at this time. Cook this mixture well for seventeen minutes on low. This will serve as your filling.

Next, slice the phyllo pastry into thin strips. Place the filling at one end of each strip, and then fold the strip to create a triangle. Fold the ingredients into the dough. Seal the phyllo pastry with wet fingers.

Repeat until you've used all the ingredients.

At this time, fill a wok half full with the olive oil (or another type of oil, if you please). Heat this oil to 375 degrees Fahrenheit. Fry the samosas for four minutes. They should be golden.

Allow the samosas to drain, and then serve the samosas warm. Enjoy!

Vegan Sundance Coleslaw

Recipe Makes 6 Servings.

Prep Time: 7 minutes.
Cook Time: 0 minutes.

Nutritional Information Per Serving: 251 calories, 20 grams carbohydrates, 17 grams fat, 6 grams protein.

Ingredients:
3 tbsp. agave syrup
1 ¼ cup cashews
½ cup sliced almonds
4 tbsp. lemon juice
1 tsp. Dijon mustard
4 cups spinach
½ cup chopped cabbage
5 parsley sprigs

Directions:
Place the agave, cashews, and the lemon juice together in a food processor. Process the ingredients well, and then add the Dijon mustard.

Next, to the side, stir together the cabbage, spinach, almonds, and the parsley sprigs. Add the above mixture, and stir well. Enjoy!

Soy and Cinnamon Appetizer Pretzels

Recipe Makes 6 Servings.

Prep Time: 5 minutes.
Cook Time: 20 minutes.

Nutritional Information Per Serving: 402 calories, 33 grams carbohydrates, 23 grams fat, 20 grams protein.

Ingredients:

4 tbsp. soy sauce
3 ½ cups pretzels
4 tbsp. agave nectar
1 tsp. ginger
3 cups almonds
1 ½ tsp. cinnamon

Directions:

Preheat the oven to 300 degrees Fahrenheit.

At this time, mix together the cinnamon, soy sauce, agave nectar, and the ginger in a medium-sized bowl. Mix the ingredients well before adding the nuts and the pretzels. Stir once more.

Next, spread the mixture out on a baking sheet. Bake the ingredients for twenty minutes, making sure to stir them every few minutes on the baking sheet.

Allow the mixture to cool, and then serve. Enjoy!

Vegan Deviled Tomatoes

Recipe Makes 6 Servings.

Prep Time: 10 minutes.
Cook Time: 0 minutes.

Nutritional Information Per Serving: 201 calories, 29 grams carbohydrates, 6 grams fat, 9 grams protein.

Ingredients:

8 ounces chickpeas
1 tsp. mustard
1/3 cup vegan mayonnaise
1 tbsp. nutritional yeast
½ tsp. curry powder
1 tbsp. lemon juice
½ tsp. salt
½ tsp. pepper
6 Roma tomatoes

Directions:

Mix together the lemon juice, mustard, vegan mayonnaise, yeast, chickpeas, pepper, and the salt in the food processor. Make sure to pulse until smooth.

Slice the tomatoes into halves, and remove the inside guts of each tomato. Stuff the tomatoes with the mixture, and serve! Enjoy!

Cashew Buttered Dates

Recipe Makes 6 Servings.

Prep Time: 5 minutes.
Cook Time: 0 minutes.

Nutritional Information Per Serving: 106 calories, 10 grams carbohydrates, 7 grams fat, 2 grams protein.

Ingredients:
6 pre-roasted cashews
1 tbsp. coconut, unsweetened and shredded
6 dates
¼ cup cashew butter

Directions:
Slice each date into halves. Remove the seeds.

Place the cashew butter on the inside of the dates, and then slice each of the roasted cashews into two pieces. Portion each half of the cashew into each half of the date.

Sprinkle the shredded coconut on top, and enjoy!

.

Spiced Vegan Crackers

Recipe Makes 6 Servings.

Prep Time: 15 minutes.
Cook Time: 35 minutes.

Nutritional Information Per Serving: 275 calories, 35 grams carbohydrates, 11 grams fat, 11 grams protein.

Ingredients:
½ tsp. xanthan gum
1 cup chickpea flour
¼ cup potato starch
¼ cup nutritional yeast
¼ cup sorghum flour
½ tsp. cumin
1 tsp. sea salt
½ tsp. curry powder
1 tsp. chili pepper powder
½ tsp. coriander
½ tsp. methi powder
½ cup water
¼ cup olive oil

Directions:

Preheat the oven to 350 degrees Fahrenheit.

Stir together all the dry ingredients in a medium-sized bowl, adding the olive oil and the water last.

As you add the oil and the water, begin working the dough with your hands. This dough should become very sticky.

Roll the dough on a floured counter, and then utilize a cookie cutter to create your crackers.

Position the crackers on your baking sheet, and bake each of the crackers for thirty-five minutes. Enjoy!

Tempeh Fries

Recipe Makes 4 Servings.

Prep Time: 5 minutes.
Cook Time: 15 minutes.

Nutritional Information Per Serving: 188 calories, 7 grams carbohydrates, 12 grams fat, 12 grams protein.

Ingredients:
1 ½ tbsp. olive oil
10 ounces tempeh, sliced into chicken-finger style portions
3 tbsp. soy sauce
1 tsp. chili pepper powder

Directions:
Pour the soy sauce and the olive oil into a skillet and heat for three minutes.

Add the tempeh to the skillet, making sure to completely coat the tempeh with the soy and olive oil sauce.

Add the chili pepper and stir. Sauté the tempeh for nine minutes, making sure that you brown each of the tempeh's sides. Enjoy!

Spiced Black Bean Dip

Recipe Makes 6 Servings.

Prep Time: 5 minutes.
Cook Time: 0 minutes.

Nutritional Information Per Serving: 125 calories, 5 grams carbohydrates, 8 grams fat, 9 grams protein.

Ingredients:
2 ½ cups black beans
2 cups salsa
1/3 cup chopped cilantro
1 tsp. cayenne
½ tsp. sea salt

Directions:
Bring all the above ingredients together into a food processor, and blend well. Season to taste, and then serve in a medium-sized serving bowl with your favorite tortilla chips. Enjoy!

Protein-Rich Tofu Dip

Recipe Makes 6 Servings.

Prep Time: 5 minutes.
Cook Time: 7 minutes.

Nutritional Information Per Serving: 88 calories, 4 grams carbohydrates, 5 grams fat, 4 grams protein.

Ingredients:
10-ounce package firm tofu
1 diced onion
2 tbsp. olive oil
4 minced garlic cloves
½ cup diced sun-dried tomatoes
Juice from 1 lemon
1/3 cup diced fresh parsley leaves
½ tsp. cumin
½ tsp. salt
½ tsp. pepper

Directions:
Heat the olive oil in a skillet over medium-high. Sauté the onions in the skillet for five minutes, and then add the

garlic. Cook the garlic and onions for an additional two minutes.

At this time, bring all the ingredients—including the garlic and the onion—together in the food processor. Process the ingredients well to create a smooth consistency. If you want something lighter, add water about a tbsp. at a time and process until smooth.

Pea and Pistachio Pesto

Recipe Makes 6 Servings.

Prep Time: 5 minutes.
Cook Time: 15 minutes.

Nutritional Information Per Serving: 173 calories, 11 grams carbohydrates, 12 grams fat, 7 grams protein.

Ingredients:
Juice from 1 lemon
1 ¼ cup diced parsley leaves
1 cup peas, frozen
1 ¼ cup pistachios, shelled
½ cup water, or less
½ tsp. sea salt
½ tsp. pepper

Directions:
Bring the frozen peas into a saucepan. Cover them with an inch of water, and cook the peas for fifteen minutes.

Bring the ingredients together in a food processor, adding the water just a bit at a time to reach your desired consistency. Process the ingredients well, and season to taste. Enjoy!

Creamy Spinach Dip

Recipe Makes 6 Servings.

Prep Time: 10 min.
Cook Time: 0

Nutritional Information Per Serving: 50 calories, 4 grams carbohydrates, 2 grams fat, 5 grams protein.

Ingredients:
1/3 cup cucumber
10-ounce package silken tofu
8 ounces spinach
1 diced onion
2 tsp. cumin
½ tsp. dried dill
½ tsp. salt
½ tsp. pepper

Directions:
After you slice the cucumber, place it on a paper towel and allow it to drain for fifteen minutes.

Next, bring the ingredients together in a food process, and process well, to your desired consistency. Enjoy!

Vegan Gouda Cheese

Recipe Makes 6 Servings.

Prep Time: 15 hours.
Cook Time: 30 minutes.

Nutritional Information Per Serving: 230 calories, 16 grams carbohydrates, 15 grams fat, 11 grams protein.

Ingredients:
½ cup nutritional yeast flakes
2 cups water
2 tbsp. agar powder
1/3 cup diced carrots
4 tbsp. lemon juice
¾ cup cashews, diced
5 tbsp. sesame tahini
½ tsp. salt
2 tsp. onion powder
1 tsp. dry mustard powder
1 tsp. turmeric
½ tsp. cumin

Directions:
Oil the bottom of a medium-sized bowl.

Next, stir together the water and the carrots in a saucepan and cook over medium-high. After the mixture begins to boil, cover the mixture and place the heat on low. Cook the carrots for a full sixteen minutes.

After sixteen minutes, add the agar powder, and bring the mixture to a boil again. After it begins to boil, decrease the heat to low once more. Allow the mixture to simmer for a full thirteen minutes at this time.

Afterwards, pour the carrots into the food processor with the remaining ingredients. Process the ingredients until it's smooth.

Bring this mixture into the oiled medium-sized bowl. Place the bowl in the fridge—uncovered—for two hours. Cover the mixture and then refrigerate it for another thirteen hours.

Serve the fake Gouda, and enjoy!

Vegan Mayonnaise (Important for Other Recipes!)

Recipe Makes 6 Servings.

Prep Time: 10 minutes.
Cook Time: 0 minutes.

Nutritional Information Per Serving: 339 calories, 2 grams carbohydrates, 37 grams fat, 1 gram protein.

Ingredients:
¾ cup soy milk
1 cup canola oil
2 tsp. lemon juice
½ tsp. mustard powder
½ tsp. salt

Directions:
Pour the lemon juice and the soy milk into a food processor. Begin to blend.

As the mixture begins to blend, pour in the oil slowly. The mixture should thicken as you pour. When it does, add the salt and the mustard, and process until smooth.

Enjoy in—and with—many of the other recipes in this book!

Southern Style Vegan Cheddar Cheese

Recipe Makes 6 Servings.

Prep Time: 8 hours.
Cook Time: 15 minutes.

Nutritional Information Per Serving: 215 calories, 22 grams carbohydrates, 11 grams fat, 10 grams protein.

Ingredients:
1 ¼ cup rice milk
¾ cup carrots
1 cup cashews
½ cup agar flakes
4 tbsp. lemon juice
½ cup nutritional yeast flakes
2 tsp. smoked paprika
1 tsp. salt
½ tsp. turmeric
½ tsp. sweet paprika

Directions:
Heat the rice milk, carrots, and cashews in a medium-sized saucepan over medium

heat. Stir well, and heat for nine minutes. At this time, the carrots should be crisp.

Next, add the agar flakes, and allow the mixture to simmer for six minutes.

At this time, pour the mixture into the food processor with the remaining ingredients. Process until you create a creamy cheese-like texture.

Bring the mixture into a bread loaf pan. Allow the mixture to refrigerate without a cover for three hours. At this time, cover the mixture, and allow it to refrigerate for five hours. Serve, and enjoy!

CHAPTER 5

VEGAN LUNCH RECIPES

Vibrant Afternoon Taco Bowl

Recipe Makes 4 Servings.

Prep Time: 6 hours (of soak time) plus 15 minutes.
Cook Time: 0 minutes.

Nutritional Information per Serving: 407 calories, 25 grams carbohydrates, 32 grams fat, 9 grams protein.

"Meat" Ingredients:
½ cup soaked walnuts (soaked for approximately six hours in water)
2 tsp. chili powder
½ tsp. salt
1 tsp. cumin
½ tsp. cayenne

"Cream" Ingredients:
1 ¼ cup cashew nuts, soaked in water for approximately six hours
4 tbsp. lemon juice
10 tbsp. water
½ tsp. salt

"Guacamole" Ingredients:

1/2 diced onion

1 avocado

1 tsp. cumin

½ chopped tomato

1 tbsp. lime juice

½ tsp. sea salt

For Serving Ingredients:

4 cups lettuce

½ cup salsa

Directions:

Begin by creating the taco meat. Pulse the initial meat ingredients in a food processor until completely mixed.
Remove the mixture and set it to the side.

Next, make the cream. Drain the nuts of their water, and add them to the food processor. Process well, adding the water as it blends. Add the lemon juice, as well. This mixture should be incredibly smooth, rather than grainy.

Next, mash up the guacamole ingredients well.

Create the bowls by placing a layer of lettuce greens in each bowl. Add the guacamole, the salsa, the taco meat, and the cream overtop. Enjoy!

Naan and Garbanzo Bean Wrap

Recipe Makes 4 Servings.

Prep Time: 5 minutes.
Cook Time: 5 minutes.

Nutritional Information Per Serving: 471 calories, 82 grams carbohydrates, 18 grams protein, 7 grams fat.

Ingredients:
4 pieces of naan bread
16 ounce can of garbanzo beans
1 diced onion
½ cup hummus
4 minced garlic cloves
1 ½ cups spinach
1 sliced cucumber
1 sliced tomato
1 tsp. cumin

Directions:
Using a potato masher or a food processor, mash together the garbanzo beans, onion, hummus, garlic, spinach, cucumber, tomato, and cumin.

Heat the naan in either a toaster oven of an oven at 350 degrees Fahrenheit for four minutes.

Portion out the ingredients into the naan wrap, and roll the naan. Enjoy at lunchtime!

Asian Broccoli Wrap

Recipe Makes 4 Servings.

Prep Time: 5 minutes.
Cook Time: 15 minutes.

Nutritional Information Per Serving: 246 calories, 33 grams carbohydrates, 8 grams fat, 14 grams protein.

Ingredients:
2 ½ cups diced broccoli
3 tbsp. soy sauce
10-ounce packaged firm tofu, pressed and released of water
4 cups sliced mushrooms
1 diced onion
2 tsp. olive oil
3 diced garlic cloves
1 tsp. ginger
8 tortillas, flour or corn

Directions:
Press at the tofu to remove all the water with a paper towel.

Bring the olive oil, mushrooms, broccoli, onions, soy sauce, and the garlic together in a skillet over medium-high heat. Cook for eight minutes, stirring constantly.

Add the garlic and the tofu at this time, and cook the mixture until the tofu is crispy. This should take about six minutes.

After the tofu is crispy, remove the mixture from the heat, and add the mixture to the flour or corn tortillas. Roll the tortillas, and enjoy!

Pumpkin Seed and Red Pepper Lettuce Wrap

Recipe Makes 6 Servings.

Prep Time: 5 minutes.
Cook Time: 10 minutes.

Nutritional Information Per Serving: 56 calories, 5 grams carbohydrates, 2 grams fat, 3 grams protein.

Ingredients:
4 tbsp. lemon juice
6 lettuce leaves
3 diced tomatoes
4 tbsp. pumpkin seeds, crushed
¾ cup diced sprouts
1 sliced red pepper
4 minced garlic cloves
1 tbsp. olive oil
1 tbsp. apple cider vinegar

Directions:
Heat olive oil over medium heat. Cook the garlic, red pepper, lemon juice, pumpkin seeds, tomatoes and the sprouts together

in a skillet. Add the apple cider vinegar, and heat on medium-high for eight minutes. The garlic should be fragrant.

Next, prepare the lettuce leaves, and portion out the ingredients into the lettuce leaves. Wrap them up, and enjoy!

Tahini and Lentil Lettuce Wraps

Recipe Makes 6 Servings.

Prep Time: 20 minutes.
Cook Time: 30 minutes.

Nutritional Information Per Serving: 371 calories, 41 grams carbohydrates, 18 grams fat, 12 grams protein.

Ingredients:

6 tortillas, whole-wheat
1 cup bulgar
¾ cup red lentils
2 cups water
3 tbsp. olive oil
2 tsp. red pepper flakes
1 diced onion
1 ¼ cup red pepper paste
½ cup tahini
2 cups cabbage, shredded

Directions:

Add the water and the red lentils to a medium-sized saucepan. Cook the mixture over medium heat, allowing them to simmer for a full twenty minutes.

Remove the saucepan from the heat. Add the bulgar, and allow the mixture to sit to the side for thirty minutes. Don't touch it.

Next, stir together the red pepper flakes, olive oil, paste, and onions. Cook the mixture in a skillet for approximately six minutes, stirring all the time.

Add this onion mixture to the lentil and bulgar, and stir well. Allow the mixture to cool before portioning it out over the whole-wheat tortillas.

Add the cabbage and the tahini over the ingredients, roll the tortillas into wraps, and enjoy!

The West Coast Hummus Wrap

Recipe Makes 4 Servings.

Prep Time:10 minutes.
Cook Time: 0 minutes.

Nutritional Information Per Serving: 283
calories, 41 grams carbohydrates, 8
grams fat, 12 grams protein.

Ingredients:
¾ cup corn, canned
4 tortillas, whole-wheat
6 tbsp. hummus
1 ¼ cup black beans, canned
1 diced tomato
1 diced and peeled avocado
1 cup diced lettuce

Directions:
Lay out each tortilla on a plate, and
portion out the above ingredients over
each tortilla. Roll the tortillas into wraps,
and enjoy!

Tofu Garlic Spring Rolls

Recipe Makes 4 Servings.

Prep Time: 10 minutes.
Cook Time: 10 minutes.

Nutritional Information Per Serving: 306 calories, 28 grams carbohydrates, 17 grams fat, 11 grams protein.

Ingredients:
12 rice papers
3 diced onions
4 tbsp. diced ginger
10-ounce package tofu, firm
4 tbsp. olive oil
9 ounces sliced mushrooms
¾ cup chopped cilantro

Directions:
Remove the tofu and press it and squeeze it to remove all the water. Dice the tofu and bring the tofu, onions, mushrooms, and garlic in a skillet over medium heat.

Cook this mixture for ten minutes, stirring every few. Add the cilantro and the ginger at this time, and allow the mixture to cook for an additional four minutes.

Next, portion out the ingredients to the rice papers. Roll the rice papers to yield small spring rolls.

Tip: you should dampen the rice papers a bit before rolling to allow them to connect well.

Homemade Vegan Flour Tortilla

Recipe Makes 6 Servings.

Prep Time: 25 minutes.
Cook Time: 5 minutes.

Nutritional Information Per Serving: 309 calories, 48 grams carbohydrates, 9 grams fat, 6 grams protein.

Ingredients:
3 cups whole wheat flour
4 tbsp. olive oil
½ tbsp. baking powder
½ tsp. salt
1 cup cold water

Directions:
Stir together the above ingredients well in a large mixing bowl.

Knead the dough with your hands to create a dough ball. Allow the dough ball to sit without touching it for fifteen minutes.

At this time, remove approximately 1/6 of the dough and roll that piece of dough into a ball. Roll out the dough into a tortilla, and then brown the tortilla in a skillet on both sides.

Repeat the above process five more times, and enjoy your vegan flour tortillas!

Quinoa and Flaxseed Cakes

Recipe Makes 6 Servings.

Prep Time: 10 minutes.
Cook Time: 25 minutes.

Nutritional Information Per Serving: 534 calories, 66 grams carbohydrates, 22 grams fat, 20 grams protein.

Ingredients:
2 cups quinoa, pre-cooked

3 tbsp. ground flax

1 ½ cups kale, chopped

7 tbsp. water

¼ cup sweet potato, grated

½ cup diced sun-dried tomatoes

½ cup sunflower seeds

½ cup oats

2 minced garlic cloves

3 tsp. red wine vinegar

5 tbsp. flour

1 tsp. salt

Directions:

Preheat the oven to 400 degrees Fahrenheit.

Stir together the water and the flax, and allow this mixture to sit to the side for seven minutes.

At this time, stir together the remaining ingredients, including the flax and the cooked quinoa. Stir the mixture well, and then shape the mixtures into patties or cakes.

Bake these patties for fifteen minutes on a cookie sheet. After fifteen minutes, flip the patties and bake for an additional nine minutes.

Cool the patties, and serve. Enjoy!

Cranberry and Lentil Meatballs

Recipe Makes 6 Servings.

Prep Time: 10 minutes.
Cook Time: 45 minutes.

Nutritional Information Per Serving: 297 calories, 21 grams carbohydrates, 19 grams fat, 13 grams protein.

Ingredients:
4 minced garlic cloves
1 ¼ cup walnuts, diced
½ cup green lentils
1 tbsp. olive oil
3 cups diced mushrooms
½ cup dried cranberries
½ cup oats, ground
½ tsp. oregano
1 tbsp. vinegar
4 tbsp. water
2 tbsp. flax
½ tsp. salt
1 cup kale

Directions:

Cook the lentils with the water, allowing them to simmer for twenty minutes.

Preheat the oven to 325 degrees Fahrenheit. Toast the walnuts in the oven for sixteen minutes. Then, boost the temperature of the oven to 350 degrees Fahrenheit.

At this time, pour the olive oil into a skillet and cook the mushrooms and the garlic. Sauté for ten minutes.

Next, add the cranberries, kale, vinegar, walnuts, and the herbs. Stir and cook for five minutes, and remove the skillet from heat.

To the side, bring together the water and the flax, and allow this mixture to sit for five minutes. Add the mixture to the skillet, then add the salt, pepper, and the oat flour.

Stir to create a sticky mixture, and then make small meatballs from the mixture. Place them on the cookie sheet, and bake them for sixteen minutes at 350 degrees Fahrenheit. Flip the meatballs, and then cook them for another fourteen minutes. Allow the meatballs to cool for four minutes before serving. Enjoy!

Asian Vegetable Bowl

Recipe Makes 6 Servings.

Prep Time: 10 minutes.
Cook Time: 30 minutes.

Nutritional Information Per Serving: 582 calories, 75 grams carbohydrates, 20 grams fat, 29 grams protein.

Ingredients:
3 cups chickpeas, canned
1 chopped head of broccoli
2 tbsp. olive oil
1 chopped head of cauliflower
½ tsp. salt
½ tsp. pepper
½ cup nutritional yeast
¾ cup cashews, soaked in water for eight hours
1 tbsp. tahini
8 tbsp. water
2 tbsp. lemon juice

Directions:

Soak the cashews in water for eight hours.

After eight hours, preheat the oven to 400 degrees Fahrenheit.

Position the broccoli and the cauliflower on a baking sheet, and add the olive oil. Place the chickpeas on the baking sheet, and cook the ingredients for sixteen minutes.

Stir the mixture, and then bake the mixture for another sixteen minutes.

While this is cooking, stir together the tahini, cashews, water, lemon juice, and the nutritional yeast. Add the mixture to a food processor, and process well.

Portion out the chickpeas and the vegetables, and then serve the bowls with the tahini sauce. Enjoy!

BBQ Chickpea Burgers

Recipe Makes 6 Burgers.

Prep Time: 5 minutes.
Cook Time: 55 minutes.

Nutritional Information Per Serving: 522 calories, 69 grams carbohydrates, 20 grams fat, 19 grams protein.

Ingredients:
1 cup garbanzo beans, uncooked
3 tbsp. sunflower seeds
2 minced garlic cloves
1 diced jalapeno
1 cup brown rice, cooked
5 tbsp. BBQ sauce
½ cup diced red pepper
½ grated carrot
¼ cup chopped parsley
3 tbsp. ground flax
1/8 cup panko breadcrumbs

Directions:
Soak the garbanzo beans for ten hours, overnight. Rinse them and simmer them

in water for a full fifty minutes.
(Alternately, buy those beans canned!)

Drain the garbanzo beans, and then bring
all the ingredients into a food processor.
Process well to make a sticky "batter."

Create burger patties with the mixture,
and then cook the patties in a skillet. Cook
them for five minutes on each side. Enjoy!

CHAPTER 6

VEGAN SLOW COOKER RECIPES

Eastern Spices Slow Cooked Lentils

Recipe Makes 6 Servings.

Prep Time: 10 minutes.
Cook Time: 3 hours.

Nutritional Information Per Serving: 401 calories, 70 grams carbohydrates, 1 gram fat, 27 grams protein.

Ingredients:
3 cups cooked lentils
1 diced bell pepper
1 peeled and diced sweet potato
1 diced onion
14 ounces tomato sauce, canned
4 minced garlic cloves
1 tsp. cumin
1 tsp. powdered ginger
½ tsp. cayenne powder
2 tsp. paprika
½ tsp. turmeric
½ tbsp. coriander
1 cup vegetable broth
juice from ½ lemon

½ tsp. salt

½ tsp. pepper

Directions:

Prepare all the vegetables.

Bring all ingredients into the slow cooker
and stir well.

Set slow cooker temperature to high and
cook for three hours.

Serve with brown rice and enjoy!

Garbanzo and Vegetable Stew

Recipe Makes 6 Servings.

Prep Time: 10 minutes.
Cook Time: 4 hours.

Nutritional Information Per Serving: 775 calories, 113 grams carbohydrates, 22 grams fat, 35 grams protein.

Ingredients:
1 diced onion
2 tsp. olive oil
30 ounces garbanzo beans
2 red potatoes, diced
4 minced garlic cloves
1-inch grated piece ginger
1 ½ tbsp. brown sugar
½ tbsp. curry powder
2 cups broth, vegetable
1 diced green pepper
1 diced red pepper
1 cauliflower head, chopped
28 ounces diced tomatoes
12 ounces spinach
10 ounces coconut milk

Directions:

Heat the olive oil in a medium-sized skillet over medium.

Add the onion, and sauté for five minutes.

Add the red potatoes and cook until the potatoes look a bit crispy. This should take about three minutes.

Add the brown sugar, curry, garlic, and ginger. Cook for thirty seconds before pouring a quarter of the vegetable broth into the skillet. Scrape the bottom of the skillet, and then pour this mixture into the slow cooker.

Add the remaining ingredients—except the coconut milk and the spinach—to the slow cooker at this time. Stir well.

Cover the slow cooker and cook on HIGH for four hours.

After four hours, add the coconut milk and the spinach. Cover the slow cooker and cook for another five minutes. Serve, and enjoy!

Apple, Squash, and Coconut Savory Chili

Recipe Makes 6 Servings.

Prep Time: 5 minutes.
Cook Time: 5 hours.

Nutritional Information Per Serving: 353 calories, 46 grams carbohydrates, 16 grams fat, 11 grams protein.

Ingredients:
2 peeled and diced apples
1 diced onion
2 peeled and diced carrots
1 chopped celery stalk
2 ½ cups diced butternut squash
14-ounce can coconut milk
14-ounce can of garbanzo beans
14-ounce can black beans
5 minced garlic cloves
½ tbsp. cumin
2 cups vegetable broth
3 tbsp. tomato paste
1 tsp. chili powder
½ tsp. salt

½ tsp. pepper

Directions:

Add the ingredients to the slow cooker and give them a good stir.

Cover the slow cooker and cook the chili on high for five hours.

With one hour left before serving, remove the lid of the slow cooker to let the chili thicken in the air. Enjoy!

Red Lentil and Sweet Potato Stew

Recipe Makes 6 Servings.

Prep Time: 10 minutes.
Cook Time: 5 hours.

Nutritional Information Per Serving: 483 calories, 96 grams carbohydrates, 19 grams protein, 1 gram fat.

Ingredients:
5 ½ cups diced and peeled sweet potatoes
1 diced onion
3 ½ cups vegetable broth
2 cups red lentils, uncooked
5 minced garlic cloves
2 tsp. garam masala
2 tsp. coriander, ground
2 tsp. chili powder
1 tsp. cayenne
14-ounce can coconut milk
¾ cup water

Directions:
Place the vegetables, broth, and the spices in the slow cooker. Cook on HIGH for

three hours. At this time, the vegetables should be soft.

Next, add the lentils and stir. Place the lid back on the slow cooker, and allow the stew to cook for an additional two hours.

At this time, add the coconut milk and the water. Stir well, and enjoy!

Slow Cooked Vegan Macaroni and Cheese

Recipe Makes 6 Servings.

Prep Time: 10 Minutes.
Cook Time: 4 Hours.

Nutritional Information Per Serving: 441 calories, 43 grams carbohydrates, 25 grams fat, 13 grams protein.

Ingredients:
8 ounces pasta, whole wheat
3 cups water
½ cup panko breadcrumbs
1 cup cashews, soaked for eight hours in water
1 ½ cup almond milk
14 ounces diced tomatoes
3 tbsp. taco seasoning
3 tbsp. nutritional yeast
2 tsp. cornstarch
1 tsp. mustard powder
1 tsp. garlic powder
1 tsp. onion powder
½ tsp. salt

½ tsp. paprika
½ tsp. pepper

Directions:
Bring water to boil in a medium-sized saucepan. Add the pasta and cook according to package directions.

Place the remaining ingredients—except the tomato and the breadcrumbs—in the food processor. Process until very smooth.

Drain the pasta. Pour cold water over it to stop its cooking.

Place the pasta in the slow cooker. Add the sauce from the food processor. Add the tomatoes and the breadcrumbs. Stir well.

Place the lid on the slow cooker, and cook on low for six hours. Every few hours, stir well. Remove the macaroni, and enjoy!

Slow Cooked Seitan Chow Mein

Recipe Makes 6 Servings.

Prep Time: 10 minutes.
Cook Time: 8 hours, 20 minutes.

Nutritional Information Per Serving: 174 calories, 30 grams carbohydrates, 1 gram fat, 10 grams protein.

Ingredients:
1 ¼ pound chopped seitan

3 chopped celery stalks

4 chopped carrots

4 chopped scallions

1 ½ cup vegetable broth

1 tsp. ginger

¾ cup soy sauce

½ cup bean sprouts

1 tsp. red pepper flakes

½ cup water

10 ounces sliced water chestnuts

¼ cup arrowroot powder

Directions:

Add all ingredients except arrowroot powder and water to the slow cooker. Stir, and cover the slow cooker. Cook the mixture on low for eight hours.

Next, add the water and the arrowroot. Cover the slow cooker half-way, and cook the chow mein for an additional twenty minutes. This way, the chow mein can thicken. Enjoy!

 **CHAPTER 7**

VEGAN SOUP
RECIPES

Vegan Lentil and Potato Soup

Recipe Makes 6 Servings.

Prep Time: 10 minutes.
Cook Time: 70 minutes.

Nutritional Information Per Serving: 347 calories, 55 grams carbohydrates, 6 grams fat, 18 grams protein.

Ingredients:

4 minced garlic cloves
1 diced onion
3 diced celery stalks
2 tbsp. olive oil
4 cups water
2 diced red potatoes
2 cups green lentils, uncooked
1 tbsp. Italian seasoning
14 ounces diced tomatoes, canned, with juices
½ cup diced cilantro

Directions:

Heat the olive oil over medium in a Dutch oven. Add the vegetables, and sauté for twelve minutes. Stir continuously.

Add the lentils, water, seasoning, and potatoes. Stir and bring the mixture to a simmer. Simmer for thirty-five minutes, covered.

Add the cilantro to the soup. Simmer the soup for twenty-five minutes.

Season to taste, and enjoy!

Barley Mushroom Soup

Recipe Makes 6 Servings.

Prep Time: 30 minutes.
Cook Time: 70 minutes.

Nutritional Information Per Serving: 232 calories, 33 grams carbohydrates, 8 grams protein, 8 grams fat.

Ingredients:
1 diced onion
3 tbsp. olive oil
30 ounces vegetable broth, organic
3 diced carrots
1 diced celery stalk
10 ounces sliced mushrooms
½ tbsp. basil, chopped
1 cup pearl barley
¼ cup chopped parsley
½ tsp. salt
½ tsp. pepper

Directions:

Heat the olive oil in a large Dutch oven. Add the vegetables, and cook for ten minutes.

Add the barley, broth, and the spices. Stir well, and allow the mixture to simmer, covered, for sixty minutes. Stir every few minutes, if possible.

Add the soymilk and season with salt and pepper. Stir.

Remove the soup from the heat and allow it to sit for thirty minutes. This way, the soup will thicken. Enjoy!

Vegan Cheesehead Broccoli Soup

Recipe Makes 6 Servings.

Prep Time: 20 minutes.
Cook Time: 40 minutes.

Nutritional information Per Serving: 100 calories, 18 grams carbohydrates, 6 grams protein, 1 gram fat.

Ingredients:
5 minced garlic cloves
½ tbsp. olive oil
½ cup diced carrots
2 diced onions
1 ½ cups chopped and peeled butternut squash
4 cups chopped broccoli
½ cup chopped celery
4 tbsp. nutritional yeast
½ tsp. cinnamon
½ tsp. salt
½ tsp. pepper

Directions:

Add the onion, garlic, and olive oil to a Dutch oven. Sauté the ingredients over medium for five minutes.

Add the remaining vegetables, and sauté for ten minutes.

Cover the pot, and cook the vegetables for another five minutes.

Add the vegetable broth. Allow the soup to simmer for twenty minutes over medium heat. Remove the Dutch oven from the heat. Allow the soup to sit for fifteen minutes.

Pour the soup into a blender, and add the nutritional yeast and the spices. Blend the soup well.

Pour the soup into the Dutch oven once more and heat through. Adjust all seasoning to taste, and enjoy!

Ginger Carrot Soup

Recipe Makes 6 Servings.

Prep Time: 30 minutes.
Cook Time: 30 minutes.

Nutritional Information Per Serving: 261 calories, 28 grams carbohydrates, 13 grams fat, 10 grams protein.

Ingredients:
1 diced onion
2 tsp. olive oil
5 minced garlic cloves
¾ cup orange juice
1 ½ pound diced carrots
4 tbsp. grated ginger
5 cups vegetable broth
1 cup cashews, soaked in water for eight hours
½ tsp. sea salt
½ tsp. pepper

Directions:

Place the cashews in a bowl of water and allow them to sit over night, at least eight hours.

Next, heat the oil in the bottom of a Dutch oven. Add the garlic and the onion, and sauté for five minutes.

Add the carrots, orange juice, broth, and ginger. Stir and allow the soup to simmer for twenty-five minutes.

Allow the soup to cool for twenty minutes.

Drain the cashews. Place the cashews in a blender, and blend.

Add the soup, and blend the soup with the cashews. Place the soup back to the Dutch oven, and season to taste. Enjoy!

Indian Spiced Broccoli Soup

Recipe Makes 6 Servings.

Prep Time: 10 minutes.
Cook Time: 30 minutes.

Nutritional information Per Serving: 615 calories, 41 grams carbohydrates, 43 grams fat, 20 grams protein.

Ingredients:
1 tsp. cumin
1 ¼ cup red lentils, uncooked
2 tsp. mustard seeds
1 diced onion
6 cups chopped broccoli
4 cups vegetable broth
4 tbsp. olive oil
1 tbsp. lemon juice
3 ½ cups almond milk
2 tsp. red pepper flakes
1 tsp. garam masala
1 tsp. turmeric

Directions:

Place the oil, onion, lentils, mustard seeds, and the cumin in a Dutch oven. Cook this mixture for ten minutes on medium-low.

Place broccoli in a food processor, and process until chunky. Pour the broccoli in the Dutch oven.

Add the broth and bring the soup to a simmer for twenty minutes, covered.

Add the almond milk, garam masala, turmeric, red pepper flakes, and lemon juice. Season to taste, and enjoy warm.

Vegan Gazpacho Soup

Recipe Makes 6 Servings.

Prep Time: 3 hours, 15 minutes.
Cook Time: 0 minutes.

Nutritional Information Per Serving: 84 calories, 15 grams carbohydrates, 3 grams protein, 1 gram fat.

Ingredients:
2 ½ pounds diced tomatoes
1 diced red pepper
1 diced cucumber
1 diced onion
3 tbsp. diced parsley
2 ½ cups tomato juice
2 diced garlic cloves
1 ½ tbsp. lime juice
1 tsp. olive oil
5 tbsp. red wine vinegar
½ tsp. salt

Directions:
Place the tomatoes, red pepper, garlic, cucumber, lime juice, onion, herbs,

tomato juice, and olive oil in a blender.
Blend until smooth.

Adjust seasoning to taste.

Chill the soup in the refrigerator for three
hours.

Serve, and enjoy!

Vegan Tortilla Soup

Recipe Makes 6 Servings.

Prep Time: 10 minutes.
Cook Time: 45 minutes.

Nutritional Information Per Serving: 232 calories, 37 grams carbohydrates, 10 grams protein, 5 grams fat.

Ingredients:
4 minced garlic cloves
1 cup quinoa, uncooked
1 tbsp. olive oil
1 diced onion
1 diced red pepper
6 corn tortillas
1 diced zucchini
30 ounces vegetable broth
1 tsp. cumin
15-ounce can diced tomatoes, with juice
½ tsp. salt
½ tsp. pepper
½ tsp. cumin

Direction:

Heat olive oil in a Dutch oven. Add the onion and the garlic, and cook for six minutes.

Add the broth, quinoa, and red pepper. Bring mixture to a boil.

Lower the heat. Allow the mixture to simmer for twenty minutes.

Slice the corn tortillas into thin strips. Heat the strips in a skillet with 1 tsp. of olive oil until toasty.

Add the cumin, zucchini, salt, and pepper to the Dutch oven. Stir, and bring the soup to a simmer for fifteen minutes.

Serve the soup warm with the tortilla strips. Enjoy!

Yukon Warm Soup Potato Soup

Recipe Makes 4 Servings.

Prep Time: 10 minutes.
Cook Time: 50 minutes.

Nutritional Information Per Serving: 208 calories, 27 grams carbohydrates, 6 grams fat, 10 grams protein.

Ingredients:
4 diced celery stalks
5 minced garlic cloves
3 tsp. coconut oil
5 cups vegetable broth
3 tsp. yellow mustard seeds
6 diced Yukon potatoes
1 tsp. cayenne pepper
1 tsp. paprika
½ tsp. chili powder
½ tsp. salt
½ tsp. pepper

Directions:

Sauté mustard seeds, garlic, and coconut oil in a large Dutch oven over medium-high.

Add the onion, and sauté for seven minutes.

Add the broth, celery, potatoes, and the spices. Stir, and allow the soup to simmer, uncovered, for forty minutes.

Bring three cups of soup into a blender. Blend until smooth.

Pour the smooth soup back into the chunky soup. Season to taste, and serve warm. Enjoy!

Vegan Tomato Soup

Recipe Makes 6 Servings.

Prep Time: 10 minutes.
Cook Time: 55 minutes.

Nutritional Information Per Serving: 298 calories, 24 grams carbohydrates, 20 grams fat, 10 grams protein.

Ingredients:
6 pounds sliced tomatoes
14 ounces coconut milk
4 garlic bulbs
1 tbsp. olive oil
1 diced onion
2 tbsp. tomato paste
2 tsp. garam masala
5 cups vegetable broth
½ tsp. salt
½ tsp. pepper

Directions:
Preheat the oven to 400 degrees Fahrenheit.

Place the tomatoes, garlic bulbs, and onion on a baking sheet. Bake the vegetables for thirty-five minutes.

Place the tomatoes, onion, and garlic in a Dutch oven. Add the tomato paste, the vegetable broth, and the coconut milk. Stir.

Add remaining seasonings and allow the soup to simmer for twenty minutes.

Pour the soup into a blender. Blend ingredients, making sure to allow the steam to escape. Serve warm, and enjoy!

Vegan Chicken Noodle Soup

Recipe Makes 4 Servings.

Prep Time: 5 minutes.
Cook Time: 35 minutes.

Nutritional information Per Serving: 230 calories, 25 grams carbohydrates, 27 grams protein, 2 grams fat.

Ingredients:
5 cups vegetable broth
1 diced celery stalk
1 diced onion
5 ounces broken fettuccine noodles
1 ¼ cup baby carrots, sliced
3 tbsp. textured vegetable protein (TVP)
2 tbsp. chopped parsley

Directions:
Pour the broth, carrots, celery, and the onion into a Dutch oven. Bring the mixture to a simmer over medium heat.

Add the fettuccine, and cover the Dutch oven. Allow it to simmer for twenty minutes.

Add the vegetable protein, cover the soup, and allow it to cook for another ten minutes.

The noodles should be tender.

Add the parsley, and serve warm. Enjoy!

 **CHAPTER 8**

VEGAN MAIN COURSE RECIPES

Easy At-Home Tempeh

Recipe Makes 6 Servings.

Prep Time: 84 Hours.
Cook Time: 35 minutes.

Nutritional Information Per Serving: 424 calories, 28 grams carbohydrates, 34 grams protein, 18 grams fat.

Ingredients:
1 ¼ pound soy beans, dried
4 tbsp. apple cider vinegar
2 tsp. tempeh starter culture (found on Amazon, Whole Foods, or your favorite natural grocery store)

Directions:
Soak the soy beans in five liters of water for twenty-four hours. Drain the beans. Rinse them.

Pour the beans in a large Dutch oven. Cover them with water once more. Add the vinegar to the beans, and bring the water to a boil.

Reduce the heat, and then allow the beans to simmer for thirty-five minutes. Drain the water.

Place the beans back in the big pot, and heat them on medium to dry them out. When they've dried, cool them completely. Add the tempeh starter culture, and stir.

Next, take 2 large, ziplock bags and stab them with needles all over to make tiny holes.

Pour the soy beans in the bags, and seal the bags. Place the bags in your home, in a warm area—in the sunlight, for example.

Allow them to sit for two and a half days—about sixty hours.

At this time, the bags are filled with white mycelium. You can lift the tempeh out of the bag in one big segment.

Store this tempeh in a sealable, clean container, and keep it in a refrigerator. Use it for future recipes!

Asian Tempeh Satay

Recipe Makes 4 Servings.

Prep Time: 5 minutes.
Cook Time: 20 minutes.

Nutritional Information Per Serving: 458 calories, 32 grams carbohydrates, 28 grams fat, 28 grams protein.

Ingredients:
1 tbsp. olive oil
4 minced garlic cloves
1 diced onion
1 sliced zucchini
4 cups diced broccoli
½ cup peanut butter
½ cup soymilk
10 ounces tempeh, sliced
4 sliced tomatoes
4 cups chopped bok choy

Directions:
Sauté the garlic and the onion in the olive oil for eight minutes in a large skillet.

Add the zucchini and the broccoli, and sauté for six minutes more.

To the side, stir together the soymilk and the peanut butter. Pour mixture into large skillet. Stir.

Add the tempeh, tomatoes, and the bok choy. Stir fry the mixture for approximately six minutes, stirring all the time. Enjoy!

Tempeh Ratatouille

Recipe Makes 6 Servings.

Prep Time: 10 minutes.
Cook Time: 25 minutes.

Nutritional Information Per Serving: 374 calories, 58 grams carbohydrates, 8 grams fat, 20 grams protein.

Ingredients:
10 ounces tempeh
15-ounce can diced tomatoes
3 cubed potatoes
10 ounces garbanzo beans
1 diced onion
2 diced carrots
3 minced garlic cloves
1 diced and peeled eggplant
1 sliced zucchini
½ tsp. rosemary, dried
½ tsp. salt
½ tsp. pepper

Directions:

Place the potatoes, carrots, and onions in a Dutch oven. Cover the vegetables in water, and bring the mixture to a boil.

Cover the Dutch oven and simmer the mixture on low for seven minutes.

Add the eggplant, broccoli, and zucchini. Simmer for three minutes. Add the vegetable broth, tomatoes, tempeh, rosemary, garlic and the garbanzo beans.

Simmer for an additional fifteen minutes, and enjoy the dinner warm. Season with salt and pepper.

Vegan's Delight Shepherd's Pie

Recipe Makes 6 Servings.

Prep Time: 20 minutes.
Cook Time: 70 minutes.

Nutritional Information Per Serving: 520
calories, 64 grams carbohydrates, 24
grams fat, 20 grams protein.

Ingredients:
1 tbsp. olive oil

1 diced onion

5 peeled and diced potatoes

3 chopped carrots

1/3 cup vegan mayonnaise (found in
appetizers and sides chapter)

1/3 cup soymilk

4 tbsp. vegan cream cheese (I used
Tofutti)

½ tsp. salt

1 tsp. Italian seasoning

1/3 cup peas, frozen

4 chopped celery stalks

3 minced garlic cloves

1 chopped tomato

14 ounces cooked and mashed lentils, used as "meat"

½ cup shredded vegan Cheddar cheese

Directions:

Place potatoes in a Dutch oven and cover them with water. Bring the water to a boil over high heat.

When it begins to boil, reduce the heat to medium-low, and simmer the potatoes until they're tender. This should take about thirty minutes.

Add the mayonnaise, soymilk, vegan cream cheese, half of the olive oil, and the salt to the potatoes, and mash at the potatoes with a potato masher. The mixture should be fluffy.

Preheat the oven to 425 degrees Fahrenheit.

Heat the other half of the olive oil in a big skillet over medium. Heat the carrots, onion, celery, peas, and the tomato for twelve minutes. Add the seasoning and the garlic. Stir well.

Place the heat on medium-low. Add the pre-mashed lentils, and cook for six minutes, stirring all the time.

Place this Boca "meat" layer at the bottom of a 9x13 inch pan. Add the potatoes overtop. Sprinkle the vegan cheese over the potatoes.

Bake the Shepherd's pie in the preheated oven for seventeen minutes.

Allow the meal to cool for a moment before slicing and serving. Enjoy!

Indiana Marrakesh Curry

Recipe Makes 6 Servings.

Prep Time: 10 minutes.
Cook Time: 40 minutes.

Nutritional Information Per Serving: 325 calories, 39 grams carbohydrates, 18 grams fat, 8 grams protein.

Ingredients:
1 chopped eggplant
1 peeled and chopped sweet potato
1 diced green pepper
1 diced red pepper
3 chopped carrots
7 tbsp. olive oil
4 minced garlic cloves
1 tbsp. curry powder
2 tsp. turmeric
1 tsp. sea salt
1 tsp. cinnamon
15 ounces chickpeas, canned and drained
1 sliced zucchini
1 tsp. cayenne pepper
¾ cup orange juice

3 tbsp. raisins
12 ounces spinach
½ medium diced onion

Directions:

Place the eggplant, sweet potatoes, peppers, onion, carrots, and half of the olive oil in a large Dutch oven. Sauté over medium-high for four minutes.

To the side, in a small saucepan, add the rest of the olive oil, the spices, and the garlic. Sauté for four minutes.

Pour the spices over the Dutch oven ingredients. Add the chickpeas, zucchini, orange juice, and the raisins.

Simmer the mixture for twenty-five minutes, covered.

Add the spinach at this time. Cook for an additional seven minutes.

Serve warm, and enjoy!

Cauliflower Italian Alfredo

Recipe Makes 6 Servings.

Prep Time: 15 minutes.
Cook Time: 60 minutes.

Nutritional information Per Serving: 300 calories, 36 grams carbohydrates, 10 grams fat, 20 grams protein.

Ingredients:
2 chopped cauliflower heads
3 minced garlic cloves
3 diced red onions

2 ½ cups soymilk, unsweetened
14 ounces cubed tofu, firm
8 ounces shredded Daiya mozzarella cheese
1/3 cup nutritional yeast
1 tbsp. marjoram, dried
3 tbsp. onion powder
1 tbsp. lemon juice
1 tbsp. dried basil
1 tsp. black pepper
1 tsp. garlic powder

4 minced kale leaves

1 ¼ cup chopped cherry tomatoes

Directions:

Preheat the oven to 350 degrees
Fahrenheit.

Place onion, garlic, and cauliflower on a
baking sheet. Bake the ingredients for
forty-five minutes.

Pour this mixture into a 9x13 inch baking
dish. Place the oven temperature down to
315 degrees Fahrenheit.

Next, blend the soymilk, vegan cheese,
tofu, onion powder, nutritional yeast,
lemon juice, spices, salt, and pepper in the
food processor. The sauce should be
creamy.

Pour the sauce into a saucepan. Cook over
medium-low for seven minutes.
Add the minced kale leaves and cook for
six minutes more.

Pour the sauce over the cauliflower. Add
the tomatoes, and stir. Bake the Alfredo in

the oven for forty minutes. It should be browned on top. Enjoy!

Greek Man's Vegan Moussaka

Recipe Makes 6 Servings.

Prep Time: 40 minutes.
Cook Time: 2 hours and 40 minutes.

Nutritional Information Per Serving: 392 calories, 64 grams carbohydrates, 10 grams protein, 12 grams fat.

Ingredients:

2 ½ pounds peeled and chopped potatoes, russet

3 minced garlic cloves

½ diced onion

1/3 cup olive oil, divided

20 ounces diced tomatoes

2 tbsp. oregano, dried

½ cup green lentils, uncooked

1 cinnamon stick

1 bay leaf

1 ½ sliced eggplants

1 ½ sliced zucchinis

2 sliced tomatoes

Directions:

Place potatoes and garlic in a large pot. Cover the potatoes with water, and boil the water for 20 minutes or until potatoes are cooked. Drain, but reserve half of the water in the pot. Add half of the olive oil and mash the potatoes with a potato masher.

Heat the remaining olive oil in a medium-sized saucepan over medium heat. Cook the onion and the oregano in the olive oil for six minutes, stirring occasionally. Add the lentils, tomatoes, cinnamon stick, bay leaf, and 2 ½ cups water.

Cover the pot, reduce the heat to medium-low, and allow the pot's mixture to simmer for fifty minutes. Toss out the cinnamon and the bay leaf.

Puree the mixture in the food processor. It should be a bit chunky.

Spread the sliced eggplant on a paper towel, and salt them. Let them stand out for forty minutes before patting them dry.

Preheat the oven to 375 degrees Fahrenheit.

Portion out half of the lentil mix into the bottom of an 8x8 inch pan. Add half of the eggplant, half of the zucchini, and half of the tomatoes overtop.

Add one half of the remaining lentil mixture over the tomatoes. Add half of the potatoes over the lentils.

Add the remaining eggplant, zucchini, and tomatoes. Top with the lentils, and then spread out the potatoes at the top.

Bake the moussaka for one hour and twenty minutes. The top should be browned. Enjoy!

Tuscan Sun Couscous

Recipe Makes 4 Servings.

Prep Time: 10 minutes.
Cook Time: 10 minutes.

Nutritional Information Per Serving: 359 calories, 53 grams carbohydrates, 7 grams fat, 21 grams protein.

Ingredients:
1 cup couscous, uncooked
3 chopped carrots
1 diced onion
½ cup thinly-sliced green pepper
½ cup thinly-sliced red pepper
3 tbsp. olive oil
½ cup chopped basil, fresh
½ tsp. salt
½ tsp. pepper
2 cups vegetable broth

Directions:
Sauté the celery, carrots, peppers, and onions in olive oil for seven minutes in a large skillet.

Add the basil, salt and pepper, and stir.

Add the couscous and the vegetable broth. Bring the broth to a boil.

Remove the mixture from the heat. Cover it, and allow it to stand for ten minutes.

Fluff up the couscous with a utensil, and enjoy.

Pesto Warm Belly Chili

Recipe Makes 4 Servings.

Prep Time: 5 minutes.
Cook Time: 20 minutes.

Nutritional Information Per Serving: 280 calories, 43 grams carbohydrates, 22 grams fat, 11 grams protein.

Ingredients:
1/3 cup olive oil
1 diced onion
3 diced carrots
14 ounces diced tomatoes
2 cups water
15 ounces chickpeas, canned
15 ounces cannellini beans, canned
15 ounces kidney beans, canned
4 tbsp. diced pine nuts
1 cup chopped parsley
½ tsp. salt
½ tsp. pepper

Directions:

Heat olive oil in a large skillet over medium-high. Add the carrots, and the onion, and cook for six minutes.

Add the tomatoes, water, salt, and pepper. Bring the mixture to a boil.

Add the beans, and cook for four minutes, stirring occasionally.

Stir together the pine nuts, garlic, parsley, and a bit of olive oil in a small mixing bowl.

Portion out the chili, and top the chili with the pesto mixture. Enjoy!

Tofu and Asparagus Curry

Recipe Makes 6 Servings.

Prep Time: 10 minutes.
Cook Time: 20 minutes.

Nutritional Information Per Serving: 359
calories, 18 grams carbohydrates, 29
grams fat, 9 grams protein.

Ingredients:
2 tbsp. olive oil
1 ¼ cup vegetable broth
12 ounces tofu, firm
2 tbsp. brown sugar
½ cup red curry paste
1 tsp. soy sauce
14-ounce can coconut milk
1 sliced red pepper
1 pound chopped asparagus

Directions:
Heat the olive oil in a large skillet over
medium-high heat. Add the tofu, and cook
for five minutes. Flip once, and cook an
additional five minutes.

Remove the tofu. Add the coconut milk and cook on medium-high. Allow the coconut milk to thicken, and then add the red curry paste. Cook for two minutes.

Add the sugar, broth, and soy sauce. The sauce will begin to simmer. When it does, add the red pepper and cook for four minutes.

At this time, add the asparagus, and cook for six minutes.

Add the tofu back to the skillet. Coat the tofu with the sauce. Cook for three minutes more.

Remove the skillet from the heat, and serve the curry warm over noodles or rice.
Enjoy!

Dinnertime BBQ Tofu Burgers

Recipe Makes 6 Servings.

Prep Time: 10 minutes.
Cook Time: 20 minutes.

Nutritional Information Per Serving: 335 calories, 48 grams carbohydrates, 13 grams fat, 6 grams protein.

Ingredients:
4 tbsp. olive oil
14 ounces extra-firm tofu
1 diced onion
3 cups vegan BBQ sauce
6 hamburger buns, I used whole wheat

Directions:
Drain the tofu, and slice the tofu into half-inch-thick pieces.

Prepare the onion.

Heat the olive oil in a skillet. Add the tofu to the skillet, and fry the tofu until it's browned.

Flip each burger, making sure to brown each side. Add the onion at this time, and cook until golden brown.

Add the BBQ sauce to the skillet, and turn the heat to low.

Place the cover on the skillet, and allow the tofu to cook on LOW for ten minutes in the barbecue sauce.

Serve the BBQ tofu on the whole-wheat hamburger buns, and enjoy!

Tofu Lasagna

Recipe Makes 6 Servings.

Prep Time: 15 minutes.
Cook Time: 60 minutes.

Nutritional Information Per Serving: 240 calories, 33 grams carbohydrates, 7 grams fat, 12 grams protein.

Ingredients:
10 ounces lasagna noodles, uncooked
14 ounces crumbled tofu
3 tbsp. soymilk
1 ¼ cup tomato sauce
2 tbsp. flax
6 tbsp. water
2 ½ cups shredded Daiya vegan mozzarella
1/3 cup Daiya vegan Parmesan cheese
½ tsp. salt
½ tsp. pepper

Directions:
Preheat the oven to 350 degrees Fahrenheit.

Boil the lasagna noodles for fifteen minutes in a large pot of water.

Place the flax and the water together, and place them to the side for five minutes.

After five minutes, stir together the flax, salt, pepper, tofu, tomato sauce, soymilk, and the mozzarella.

Place a small layer of the mixture at the bottom of a 9x13 inch pan.

Then, follow this layer with a layer of lasagna noodles.

Follow the lasagna with the sauce.

Do this until you run out of ingredients, and then top the lasagna with the Parmesan cheese.

Bake the lasagna for thirty-eight minutes. Serve the lasagna warm, and enjoy!

Vibrant Vegan Stroganoff

Recipe Makes 6 Servings.

Prep Time: 10 minutes.
Cook Time: 40 minutes.

Nutritional Information Per Serving: 487 calories, 51 grams carbohydrates, 25 grams fat, 18 grams protein.

Ingredients:

14 ounces spaghetti noodles
4 tbsp. vegan sour cream
18 ounces tofu, firm
14 ounces coconut milk
1 tbsp. olive oil
4 diced onions, small
2 tbsp. soy sauce
10 ounces sliced mushrooms
3 minced garlic cloves

Directions:

Place the spaghetti noodles in a large pot of water and boil for ten minutes.

Drain the pot.

Heat olive oil in a skillet over medium. Sauté the tofu in the olive oil for twelve minutes, stirring constantly. After twelve minutes, set the tofu to the side.

Place the mushrooms, onions, soy sauce, and the garlic in a skillet. Heat for ten minutes.

Stir together the coconut milk and the vegan sour cream. Pour this mixture into the skillet, and cook for three minutes, stirring occasionally.

Add the tofu back to the skillet. Cook for six additional minutes.

Pour this mixture over the spaghetti noodles, and serve. Enjoy!

Lentil Taco Meat

Recipe Makes 6 Servings.

Prep Time: 10 minutes.
Cook Time: 50 minutes.

Nutritional Information Per Serving: 415 calories, 24 grams carbohydrates, 29 grams fat, 18 grams protein.

Ingredients:
1 cup green lentils, uncooked
2 cups walnuts, diced, toasted
2 tsp. oregano
2 tsp. chili powder
2 tbsp. olive oil
4 tbsp. water

Directions:
Cook lentils in a pot of water. Bring the water to a boil at medium-high. Reduce the heat, and simmer the lentils for thirty minutes.

While the lentils are cooking, preheat the oven to 300 degrees Fahrenheit. Bake the walnuts on a baking sheet for sixteen minutes. Afterwards, allow the walnuts to cool.

Stir the lentils and the walnuts together. Add the spices and a small amount of water. (You can add less than the 4 tbsp., if the consistency is right for taco meat.)

Fill your corn tortillas with the lentil taco meat, and enjoy!

Vegan Stuffed Shells

Recipe Makes 4 Servings.

Prep Time: 10 minutes.
Cook Time: 50 minutes.

Nutritional Information Per Serving: 600 calories, 44 grams carbohydrates, 16 grams protein, 41 grams fat.

Ingredients to Make Vegan Ricotta:
3 minced garlic cloves
3 cups cashews, soaked for eight hours in water
3 tbsp. apple cider vinegar
½ cup crumbled tofu
2 tbsp. lemon juice
1 cup diced kale
1 tsp. oregano

Ingredients for Shells:
15 pasta shells
3 ½ cups marinara sauce
2 tbsp. olive oil

Directions:

Preheat the oven to 350 degrees Fahrenheit.

Puree the garlic, cashews, apple cider vinegar, tofu, lemon juice, kale, and oregano in a food processor. Season to taste. Set this mixture to the side.

Boil the pasta shells until they're al dente, approximately twelve minutes.

Pour marinara sauce into the bottom of a 9x13 inch pan.

Scoop the filling into the shells. Place the shells at the bottom of the baking dish, and add more marinara and olive oil over them.

Bake the shells for thirty-five minutes, and allow them to cool. Serve, and enjoy!

Butternut Squash-Based Linguine

Recipe Makes 4 Servings.

Prep Time: 10 minutes.
Cook Time: 45 minutes.

Nutritional Information Per serving: 421 calories, 66 grams carbohydrates, 12 grams fat, 14 grams protein.

Ingredients:
2 ½ pounds diced butternut squash
4 tbsp. olive oil
4 minced garlic cloves
2 tbsp. chopped sage
4 cups vegetable broth
1 diced onion
½ tsp. red pepper flakes
16 ounces linguine

Directions:
Heat the olive oil and the sage in a large skillet over medium-high heat for five minutes.

Add the garlic, onion, squash, and red pepper. Stir. Cook for ten minutes, stirring occasionally.

Next, add the vegetable broth to the mixture and simmer it for twenty minutes on medium heat.

In a large pot to the side, boil the pasta for approximately ten minutes, until al dente. Drain the pasta, keeping one cup of water at the bottom of the large pot.

Pour the squash mixture into a blender, and blend until smooth.

Pour this mixture over the pasta and the reserved water in the large pot.

Cook the mixture for three additional minutes. Salt and pepper, and serve warm.
Enjoy!

Sweet Potato and Garbanzo Basil Burgers

Recipe Makes 6 Servings.

Prep Time: 20 minutes.
Cook Time: 30 minutes.

Nutritional Information Per Serving: 351 calories, 56 grams carbohydrates, 16 grams protein, 8 grams fat.

Ingredients:
1 sweet potato, grated
1 tbsp. olive oil
3 minced garlic cloves
¼ cup chopped basil
2 tsp. chopped ginger
¼ cup chopped cilantro
¾ cup oat flour
1 tbsp. flax
3 tbsp. water
15 ounces garbanzo beans
1 tsp. coriander
2 tsp. lime juice
½ tsp. sea salt

Directions:

Preheat the oven to 375 degrees Fahrenheit.

Place the flax and the water together in a bowl and allow them to rest, untouched, for five minutes.

Grate the sweet potato, and place it in a mixing bowl. Toss with olive oil.

Add the garlic, basil, ginger, cilantro, coriander, and oat flour. Stir well.

Process the garbanzo beans in a food processor. Add the beans to the mixture, and stir.

Pour the flax mixture to the large bowl, and stir well.

Add the lime juice and the salt. Stir.

Form the mixture into 6 patties. Place the patties on the baking sheet, and bake them for eighteen minutes.

Flip the patties, and bake them for an additional twelve minutes. Enjoy the burgers!

Homemade Seitan: Extra Boost of Organic Protein

Recipe Makes 6 Servings.

Prep Time: 8 hours.
Cook Time: 40 minutes.

Nutritional Information Per Serving: 483 calories, 100 grams carbohydrates, 14 grams protein, 1 gram fat.

Ingredients:
6 cups flour, whole-wheat
2 ½ cups chilled water

1 diced onion
4 ½ cups water
1/3 cup soy sauce
1 diced tomato
1 ½ tbsp. miso paste
4 minced garlic cloves

Directions:
Stir together flour and chilled water in a large mixing bowl. Stir until dough is formed.

Mold the dough into a ball. Place the ball in a large bowl of very cold water. Cover the dough and let the bowl sit in the refrigerator for eight hours.

Next, remove the dough from the water, and rinse it. Knead at the dough and release all the water.

Slice the dough into small pieces.

To the side, stir together the remaining ingredients: water, onion, tomato, soy sauce, miso paste, and garlic. Add the mixture to a saucepan and bring the mixture to a boil.

Drop each small piece of the seitan into the boiling mixture. Bring the mixture back to a boil.

Place the heat on LOW. Allow the broth to simmer for thirty-five minutes.

Remove the onion and the tomato from the broth, and throw them away.

Keep the seitan in the broth, and keep the broth in the refrigerator for future use.

Organic Seitan "Fried Chicken"

Recipe Makes 6 Servings.

Prep Time: 10 minutes.
Cook Time: 10 minutes.

Nutritional Information Per Serving: 382 calories, 20 grams carbohydrates, 14 grams protein, 25 grams fat.

Ingredients:
1 ¼ pound seitan, sliced and diced
1 tsp. garlic powder
1 tsp. onion powder
1 tsp. cayenne powder
½ cup mustard
2 cups almond flour
2 tbsp. baking powder
½ cup nutritional yeast
1/3 cup water
Olive oil for cooking

Directions:
Stir together the spices, yeast, and almond flour in a shallow bowl.

In another bowl, stir together the water and the mustard. Add one half of the flour mixture to the mustard, and stir.

Coat the seitan first with the mustard, then with the spices.

Heat the olive oil in a large skillet over medium-high heat.

Cook the seitan for five minutes on each side.

Serve with your favorite vegan sauce, and enjoy!

CHAPTER 9

VEGAN DESSERT RECIPES

Super Chocolate Vegan Cookies

Recipe Makes 24 Servings.

Prep Time: 10 minutes.
Cook Time: 12 minutes.

Nutritional Information Per Serving: 221 calories, 21 grams carbohydrates, 13 grams fat, 4 grams protein.

Ingredients:

1/3 cup cane sugar

1 tsp. vanilla

1 tbsp. ground flax

½ cup brown sugar

½ cup sunflower seed butter

2 cups oat flour

4 tbsp. water

½ cup coconut oil, melted

2 tsp. soy milk

14 ounces chopped non-dairy chocolate

½ tsp. baking powder

½ tsp. baking soda

Directions:

Preheat the oven to 350 degrees Fahrenheit.

Stir together the flax and the water, and then set these ingredients to the side for six minutes without touching them.

Next, bring the vanilla, cane sugar, brown sugar, seed butter, and the coconut oil into large mixing bowl. Add the flax seed, and stir well.

Add the dry ingredients to the mixture at this time, and stir well.

Add the soy milk at the end of your mixing time in order to wet the dough a bit. Stir well.

Add the chocolate last, and stir well.

Next, create the small cookie dough balls and place them on a baking sheet. Flatten them a bit before cooking, and bake them for a full twelve minutes.

Cool the cookies, and enjoy!

Vegan Pumpkin Bars

Recipe Makes 12 Servings.

Prep Time: 15 minutes.
Cook Time: 22 minutes.

Nutritional Information Per Serving: 170
calories, 24 grams carbohydrates, 6
grams fat, 3 grams protein.

Ingredients:
3 tbsp. water
1 tbsp. flax seed
¾ cup pumpkin puree, canned
1 cup date sugar
½ tsp. sea salt
2 tsp. vanilla
1 tsp. ginger
½ tsp. baking soda
½ tsp. nutmeg
1 cup oat flour
1 cup almond flour
1 cup oats
1 tbsp. arrowroot powder
1/3 cup diced pecans
4 tbsp. vegan chocolate chips

Directions:

Preheat the oven to 350 degrees Fahrenheit.

Add the flax seed and the water to a bowl, and allow the mixture to sit to the side for six minutes. Do not touch it.

Stir together the sugar and the pumpkin. Add the flax mixture and the vanilla. Stir well. Add the spices, salt, and baking soda.

Next, add the almond flour, oat flour, arrowroot powder, oats, and the pecans. Stir well.

Spread the dough in a baking pan. Press the chocolate chips into the top.

Bake the dough for twenty-two minutes. Remove the pan and allow it to cool. Slice into bars, and enjoy.

Vegan Ginger Cookies

Recipe Makes 12 Cookies.

Prep Time: 10 minutes.
Cook Time: 11 minutes.

Nutritional Information Per Serving: 190 calories, 33 grams carbohydrates, 3 grams protein, 6 grams fat.

Ingredients:
3 tbsp. water
1 tbsp. flax
3 tbsp. molasses
1/3 cup vegan butter (I used Earth Balance)
1 tsp. cinnamon
3 tbsp. maple syrup
½ cup date sugar
1 tsp. ginger
2 cups spelt flour
3 tbsp. sugar
½ cup diced ginger, candied
½ tsp. baking powder

Directions:

Preheat the oven to 374 degrees
Fahrenheit.

Make the flax egg by stirring together the
water and the flax. Set the mixture to the
side and allow it to sit for five minutes.

Stir together the flax, vegan butter, sugar,
molasses, and the syrup. Add the dry
ingredients. Stir well.

Next, add the candied ginger.

Roll into 12 cookie balls, and roll them
over the 3 tbsp. sugar. Place the cookies
on a cookie sheet, and flatten them
slightly.

Bake the cookies for eleven minutes.
Allow the cookies to cool before serving.

Vegan Oatmeal Raisin Cookies

Recipe Makes 24 Cookies.

Prep Time: 10 minutes.
Cook Time: 12 minutes.

Nutritional Information Per Serving: 93 calories, 16 grams carbohydrates, 3 grams fat, 1 gram protein.

Ingredients:
¾ cup whole wheat flour
1 tsp. cinnamon
½ tsp. baking soda
½ tsp. salt
½ cup applesauce
1/3 cup date sugar
3 tbsp. maple syrup
½ cup brown sugar
1 tsp. vanilla
1/3 cup raisins
¼ cup olive oil
2 cups oats

Directions:

Preheat the oven to 375 degrees Fahrenheit.

Stir together the dry ingredients.

Stir together the wet ingredients in a large mixing bowl. Add the dry ingredients to the wet ingredients.

Stir well, and then add the oats and the raisins. Stir until combined.

Chill the batter in the fridge for thirty minutes.

Drop the cookies on a baking sheet. Bake them for twelve minutes. Enjoy!

Carrot Cake Vegan Muffins

Recipe Makes 20 Muffins.

Prep Time: 8 minutes.
Cook Time: 20 minutes.

Nutritional Information Per Serving: 125 calories, 17 grams carbohydrates, 5 grams fat, 3 grams protein.

Ingredients:
¾ cup date sugar
1 ½ cup whole-wheat flour
Zest from 1 orange
1 tsp. cinnamon
1 tsp. baking soda
2 cups bran flakes
½ cup diced walnuts
1 ¼ cup grated carrots
½ cup raisins
1 ½ cups almond milk
½ cup avocado oil
1 tsp. apple cider vinegar

Directions:

Preheat the oven to 400 degrees Fahrenheit.

Stir together the dry ingredients in a big mixing bowl.

Mix together wet ingredients in a small mixing bowl. Add the wet ingredients to the dry ingredients.

Stir slowly, making sure not to over mix.

Fill the muffin tins, and bake the muffins for twenty minutes. Cool and enjoy!

Chocolate Zucchini Bread

Recipe Makes 6 Servings.

Prep Time: 8 minutes.
Cook Time: 30 minutes.

Nutritional Information Per Serving: 310 calories, 65 grams carbohydrates, 3 grams fat, 8 grams protein.

Ingredients:
1 cup applesauce
2 tbsp. flax
6 tbsp. water
1 cup date sugar
1 ¾ cup flour
½ cup cocoa powder
1 tbsp. cinnamon
2 tsp. vanilla
2 cups grated zucchini
1 cup non-dairy chocolate chips
½ tsp. sea salt

Directions:
Preheat the oven to 325 degrees Fahrenheit.

Add the water to the flax seed, and set the mixture to the side for five minutes.

Stir together the flour, cocoa powder, and cinnamon. Add the applesauce, flax, date sugar, vanilla, grated zucchini, chocolate chips, and salt. Stir well.

Spread the batter in a bread loaf pan. Bake the mixture for twenty-eight minutes.

Cool the zucchini chocolate bread, and enjoy!

Avocado Chocolate Mousse

Recipe Makes 6 Servings.

Prep Time: 4 hours and 10 minutes.
Cook Time: 0 minutes.

Nutritional Information Per Serving: 431 calories, 36 grams carbohydrates, 34 grams fat, 5 grams protein.

Ingredients:
5 avocadoes
¾ cup cocoa powder
2 ½ tsp. vanilla
½ cup coconut palm sugar
½ tsp. sea salt

Directions:
Peel and pit the avocadoes. Place the meat in the food processor.

Add the cocoa powder, vanilla, coconut palm sugar, and the salt to the food processor and process until smooth.

Place the ingredients in a closable container, and chill the mousse for four hours.
Enjoy!

Kid's Vegan Monkey Bread

Recipe Makes 12 Servings.

Prep Time: 15 minutes.
Cook Time: 30 minutes.

Nutritional Information Per Serving: 200 calories, 25 grams carbohydrates, 10 grams fat, 3 grams protein.

First Round Ingredients:
1 ¾ cup whole-wheat flour
¼ cup date sugar
½ tbsp. baking powder
5 tbsp. Earth Balance butter
½ tsp. salt

Second Round Ingredients:
1 cup soymilk
¾ cup non-dairy chocolate chips

Third Round Ingredients:
2 tsp. cinnamon
½ tsp. nutmeg
½ cup date sugar
4 tbsp. Earth Balance, melted

Directions:

Preheat the oven to 350 degrees Fahrenheit.

Stir together the whole wheat flour, date sugar, baking powder, Earth Balance butter, and salt—all from the first round. (Make sure to cut the butter into the mixture. You'll end up with a dough.)

Stir together the soymilk and the non-dairy chocolate chips. Stir this mixture into the first mixture.

With your hands, make twelve dough balls. Place them in a bread pan. They should touch each other.

Drizzle the dough balls with the melted Earth Balance from the third round.

To the side, stir together the cinnamon, nutmeg, and date sugar. Sprinkle this over the monkey bread.

Bake the monkey bread for twenty-nine minutes. The bread should cool before serving. Enjoy!

Vegan Chocolate Cream Pie

Recipe Makes 12 Servings.

Prep Time: 5 hours and 30 minutes.
Cook Time: 0 minutes.

Nutritional Information Per Serving: 441 calories, 41 grams carbohydrates, 28 grams fat, 5 grams protein.

Crust Ingredients:
2 ½ cups flour, all-purpose
1 cup Earth Balance butter
4 tsp. date sugar
7 tbsp. cold water
½ tsp. sea salt

Filling Ingredients:
½ cup date sugar
1/3 cup cornstarch
4 tbsp. cocoa powder
1 cup coconut milk, full-fat
1 cup almond milk
1 tsp. vanilla
10 ounces Vegan Whipped Cream
6 ounces diced dark chocolate, non-dairy

Directions:

Preheat the oven to 425 degrees Fahrenheit.

Stir together the flour, date sugar, and sea salt. Add the Earth Balance, cutting it into the mixture to make a crumble.

Add the cold water to the mixture and stir. This is the crust dough.

Roll the dough into a pie plate, and bake the dough for twenty-four minutes.

Whisk together the date sugar, cornstarch, cocoa powder, coconut milk, almond milk, vanilla, Vegan Whipped Cream, and the dark chocolate pieces.

Add the mixture to a medium-sized saucepan, and head over medium. Stir continuously.

Pour the ingredients into the piecrust. Cover the pie, and chill it for five hours. Serve, and enjoy!

Vegan Apple and Apricot Cobbler

Recipe Makes 6 Servings.

Prep Time: 10 minutes.
Cook Time: 40 minutes.

Nutritional Information Per Serving: 349 calories, 42 grams carbohydrates, 18 grams fat, 4 grams protein.

Filling Ingredients:
2 tbsp. arrowroot powder
3 ½ cups sliced apples
5 cups sliced apricots
1/3 cup date sugar
1 tsp. vanilla
1 tsp. cinnamon
½ cup water

Biscuit Ingredients:
¾ cup ground oats
¾ cup almond flour
2 tsp. baking powder
½ tsp. salt
1/3 cup soymilk
1 tbsp. date sugar

5 tbsp. Earth Balance
1 tsp. cinnamon

Directions:
Preheat the oven to 400 degrees
Fahrenheit.

Stir the apricots, apples, sugar, arrowroot,
cinnamon, vanilla, and the water together
in a large bowl.

Pour the ingredients into a saucepan, and
heat over medium-high.

Bring the mixture to boil. At this time,
reduce the heat to medium-low, and
simmer the ingredients for five minutes.

Remove the mixture from the heat. Add
vanilla, and stir.

Add the biscuit's dry ingredients to a
small bowl: oats, flour, baking powder,
salt, date sugar, and the cinnamon.

Add the Earth Balance, and cut the butter
to create a crumble.

Add the soymilk. Stir well.

Next, pour the apple and apricot mixture into a 9x13 baking dish. Pour the biscuit topping over the apples and apricots.

Bake the mixture for thirty-two minutes in the preheated oven.

Serve the apple and apricot crisp warm, and enjoy!

Vegan Coconut Cake

Recipe Makes 12 Servings.

Prep Time: 10 minutes.
Cook Time: 30 minutes.

Nutritional Information Per Serving: 394 calories, 37 grams carbohydrates, 26 grams fat, 5 grams protein.

Ingredients:
2 ½ cups almond milk
1 ½ cups coconut, unsweetened and shredded
1 cup coconut flour, toasted
4 tsp. flax meal
2 tsp. apple cider vinegar
2 tsp. vanilla
4 tsp. baking powder
1 tsp. baking soda
1 ¾ cup flour
2 tsp. vanilla
¾ cup coconut palm sugar
1 tsp. sea salt
½ cup melted coconut oil

Directions:

Preheat the oven to 375 degrees Fahrenheit.

Stir together the flax, almond milk, and the apple cider.

To the side, stir together the flour, coconut flour, baking soda, and baking powder.

Add the coconut sugar, coconut oil, salt, and vanilla to this second flour-based bowl. Stir well.

Add the flax, almond milk, and apple cider, and stir well.

Pour the batter into 2 8-inch cake pans. Bake the cakes for twenty-nine minutes.

Cool the cakes, and frost—with the following vegan cake frosting!

Vegan Buttercream Frosting

Recipe Makes 6 Servings.

Prep Time: 8 minutes.
Cook Time: 0 minutes.

Nutritional Information Per Serving: 431 calories, 60 grams carbohydrates, 21 grams fat, 1 gram protein.

Ingredients:
1/3 cup margarine, non-hydrogenated
1/3 cup non-hydrogenated shortening
1 tsp. vanilla
3 cups powdered sugar
1/3 cup soymilk, unsweetened

Directions:
Beat margarine and shortening together until fluffy.

Add the powdered sugar and beat for an additional four minutes.

Add the soymilk and the vanilla.

Beat for five minutes. The mixture should be fluffy.

Enjoy over your favorite cakes!

Sweet Cashew Bar with Chocolate Chips

Recipe Makes 6 Servings.

Prep Time: 80 minutes.
Cook Time: 0 minutes.

Nutritional Information Per Serving: 191 calories, 21 grams carbohydrates, 11 grams fat, 4 grams protein.

Ingredients:
1 cup cashews
½ tsp. vanilla
½ cup diced dates
3 tbsp. dark chocolate chips, non-dairy
½ tsp. sea salt

Directions:
First, place the cashews and the salt in the food processor.

Process until crumbly.

Add the diced dates. Process for another twenty seconds to create a sticky consistency.

Next, add the chocolate chips and the vanilla. Process once more.

Place the mixture in an 8x8 inch pan, and spread it evenly.

Freeze the bars for one hour before slicing them up! Enjoy!

Vegan Chocolate and Almond Fudge

Recipe Makes 24 Squares.

Prep Time: 2 hours, 20 minutes.
Cook Time: 0 minutes.

Nutritional Information Per Serving: 50 calories, 5 grams carbohydrates, 3 grams fat, 1 gram protein.

Ingredients:
1/3 cup maple syrup
¼ cup melted coconut oil
¼ cup almond butter
1/3 cup cocoa powder
1 cup diced walnuts
1 tbsp. vanilla
½ tsp. sea salt

Directions:
Melt the coconut oil over low in a small saucepan.

After it's melted, bring it together with the almond butter in a mixing bowl.

Add the maple syrup, cocoa powder, vanilla, and salt. Stir well until smooth. Then, add the walnuts. Pour the batter into a bread pan.

Freeze the fudge for two hours. Slice and serve. Enjoy!

Grandma's Homemade Tapioca Pudding

Recipe Makes 4 Servings.

Prep Time: Overnight + 10 minutes.
Cook Time: 30 minutes.

Nutritional Information Per Serving: 330 calories, 28 grams carbohydrates, 25 grams fat, 3 grams protein.

Ingredients:
1 cup coconut milk
2 ½ cups almond milk
½ cup tapioca pearls
½ cup agave syrup
1 ½ tbsp. water
2 tsp. vanilla
½ tsp. sea salt

Directions:
Soak the tapioca in ½ cup of almond milk overnight.

Soak the cornstarch with the water overnight, as well.

Next, pour the rest of the almond milk to the tapioca. Pour this mixture into a saucepan and heat over medium.

When the mixture begins to boil, add the coconut milk, vanilla, and agave. Cook for eighteen minutes, making sure to stir all the time.

Next, add the cornstarch with water and a bit of salt. Stir and cook for another five minutes.

Cool the pudding at room temperature or in the refrigerator for two hours prior to serving. Enjoy!

Conclusion

Beginning the vegan lifestyle means so many things for your waistline, your physical health, and the way you look at the world around you.

For example: when you adopt the vegan lifestyle, you bring an automatic adjustment to how you interact with the world. You understand that every action, every decision you make alters something in the world. Ultimately, you live in greater harmony with the external environment. You live knowing that you're not harming animals; you aren't harming the earth.

Furthermore, the vegan lifestyle brings all the nutrients and vitamins your body requires in order to live well. You can refute the terrorizing elements that currently lurk in everyday American foods, things that ultimately put you at risk for serious diseases like cancers and heart disease. You can skim back on your toxin consumption and live well.

So with the help of this book, you can take small steps into the vegan lifestyle, one recipe at a time. Each is pulsing with wholesome and delightful nutrients; each is designed to bring wellness and overall health.

Remember that the vegan lifestyle allows you to live with eternal care and harmony with the outside world. Don't allow yourself to accept anything less.

17725278R00134

Printed in Great Britain
by Amazon